MOON

MOON

STEWART ROSS

SCHOLASTIC

Oxford University Press is a department of the University of Oxford. It furthers
the University's objective of excellence in research, scholarship, and education
by publishing worldwide in Oxford New York Auckland Cape Town
Dar es Salaam Hong Kong Karachi Mexico City Nairobi New Delhi
Shanghai Taipei Toronto

With offices in Argentina Austria Brazil Chile Czech Republic France
Greece Guatemala Hungary Italy Japan Poland Portugal Singapore
South Korea Switzerland Thailand Turkey Ukraine Vietnam

ISBN-13: 978-0-545-12732-5
ISBN-10: 0-545-12732-7

10 9 8 7 6 5 4 3 2 1   09 10 11 12 13

Originated by Oxford University Press
Created by White-Thomson Publishing Ltd.

Designer: Robert Walster
Original editor: Sonya Newland

Printed in Malaysia for Imago
First American edition, January 2009

Key to spreads:

- Moon Landing
- Moon Facts
- Moonstruck
- Information

CONTENTS

INTRODUCTION

Forty years ago something magical happened — a dream came true. A man walked on the Moon. Nor was that all: Having flown into space and carried out his mission, he and his two colleagues returned safely to Earth. Truly, it was the greatest adventure, the most tremendous enterprise ever undertaken by the human race.

This book commemorates that achievement. It does so by tracing the story of what has become known as the "Space Race," in which two mighty powers strove to outwit and outperform each other. Out of this struggle was born the *Apollo* program, and from that program emerged *Columbia*, *Eagle*, and the giant leap for mankind.

These pages have a broader mission than just retelling a famous story. They seek to put that story into its scientific and cultural context. Just what was this "Moon" that Neil Armstrong planted his foot on? How was it made? What did it consist of and what was its relation to planet Earth?

The *Eagle* did not land against a purely scientific backdrop, either. Since the beginning of time, humans have been in awe of the Moon, worshipping it, painting it, writing about it, and even howling to it. Throughout history and prehistory, there has been no more powerful influence on our culture.

Therein lies the wonder of *Apollo 11*. It was not simply a scientific triumph or human achievement. Rather it was a manifestation of the human spirit in all its bewildering glory.

Stewart Ross

COUNTDOWN

10

For thousands of years
it was an impossible madness . . .

9

A dream. . . .

8

Then science made it a fiction,

7

A vague possibility,

6

Which manned flight made realistic

5

and rockets made practicable. . . .

4

So it became a goal,

3

A race . . .

2

Until, at 09:32 on July 16, 1969,

1

It finally happened. . . .

↑ *Apollo 11*'s official badge, known as a patch.

LIFTOFF!

This was the moment of supreme danger. In their tiny module at the tip of the gigantic *Saturn V* rocket sat three astronauts. Below them lay smoking tanks packed with thousands of tons of rocket fuel and liquid oxygen.

TARGET: MOON

"All engines running!" Sheets of red, orange, and white flame spewed forth from the five enormous engines, surging hundreds of feet to the side and driving thick clouds of smoke and dust into the warm Florida air.

A leak, the smallest spillage, a careless check or faulty calculation — one error and the rocket would transform instantly into a colossal bomb capable of vaporizing the rocket and the steel of the gantry, destroying the launchpad, and incinerating the surrounding landscape. The astronauts would not even have time to cry out. For a few heart-stopping moments, as the engines strained and roared, the ground shook, and around the world millions watched on television in silent awe. It looked as if the task of raising 3,307 tons (3,000 tonnes) of rocket into the air was too great, even for those massive engines.

"Liftoff! We have liftoff!" The relief in the voice of the NASA official was almost tangible. Slowly, incredibly slowly at first, the rocket rose from the ground. The gantry arms swung back. "Thirty-two minutes past the hour, liftoff on *Apollo 11*!" cried the commentator. Then, seconds later, "Gantry cleared!"

One of the greatest missions in human history was underway. *Apollo 11* was going to the Moon.

↑ The *Apollo 11* crew checks mission details over breakfast.
← The Moon men: Neil Armstrong, Michael Collins, and Buzz Aldrin.

THE *APOLLO* PROGRAM

By the summer of 1969 the *Apollo* program had been in place for eight years. It began in May 1961, when US President John F. Kennedy announced confidently, "I believe that this nation should commit itself to achieving the goal, before this decade is out, of landing a man on the Moon and returning him safely to the Earth." It was a tall order. The first American in space, Alan B. Shepard (1923–98), had made his voyage only twenty days earlier.

⬆ US President John F. Kennedy, the politician who launched the Moon mission.

America's National Aeronautics and Space Administration (NASA) was made responsible for the program and given a massive boost in funds and personnel. During the 1960s, the first 10 *Apollo* missions tested every step of the journey except the last — that of actually putting a human being on the surface of the Moon. This was the momentous task of Neil Armstrong (b. 1930), Michael Collins (b. 1930), and Buzz Aldrin (b. 1930), the astronauts in the *Saturn V* rocket that was now gathering speed on its famous journey.

◑ Blastoff! *Saturn V* heads skyward from its launchpad.

THE MOON

But what exactly is the Moon? The second-brightest object in our sky, and the Earth's only natural satellite, looks round. Actually, it bulges on the side nearest to us. Even with the naked eye we can make out the lumps and bumps on its surface: For billions of years, having no atmosphere to protect it, the Moon has been bombarded with debris from outer space. Crashing in at great speed, this debris has left a maze of Moon craters.

⬆ Just about every newspaper in the world made the Moon landing its headline story.

⬇ Some impact: The crater known as "Limb of Copernicus" is a staggering 61 miles (98 km) wide!

The New York Times

MEN WALK ON MOON
ASTRONAUTS LAND ON PLAIN; COLLECT ROCKS, PLANT FLAG

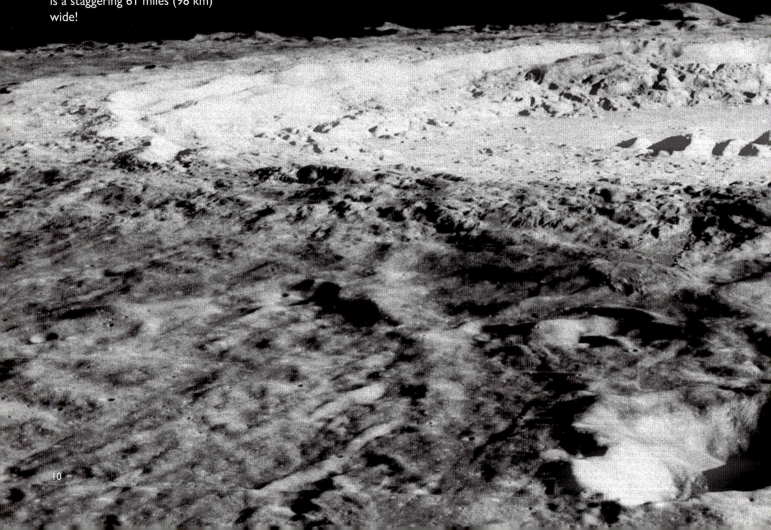

MOON MAKING

Only fairly recently have scientists worked out for certain how the Moon was formed. Around 4.6 billion years ago, before the Earth was really solid, a slightly smaller but similar object bumped into it. It was not a head-on collision but a glancing blow, after which the smaller object spun off into space. The debris created by this galactic accident went into an eccentric orbit about 238,855 miles (384,400 km) from the Earth. Over time it came together to form the Moon.

IRON AND WATER

The collision theory explains why the Moon contains so little iron, the main ingredient of the Earth's core. The bits and pieces that formed the Moon came from the outer layers of the Earth and the object that hit it. The water on the Moon's surface (a tiny amount in the form of ice) probably arrived with incoming comets and meteoroids.

DUSTY DEATH

With a radius of 1,080 miles (1,738 km), the Moon is much smaller than the Earth and has only one-sixth of its gravity. That is why astronauts on its surface can leap huge distances. It has almost no atmosphere, certainly no oxygen, and it has never hosted any form of life. Temperatures on the surface range from a scalding 253°F (123°C) in the sunlight to a super-chilling -387°F (-233°C) in the dark. The battered and rocky surface is thick with dust.

As the Earth turns, the Moon's gravity causes our seas to surge with tides. The Moon rotates at the same rate as it orbits the Earth, so we always see the same sunlit face; whether this is full Moon, half-Moon, or another phase depends on the alignment of the Sun, Earth, and the Moon. With the Moon circling the Earth once every 27.322 days, it is not surprising that it became the basis of the first calendars.

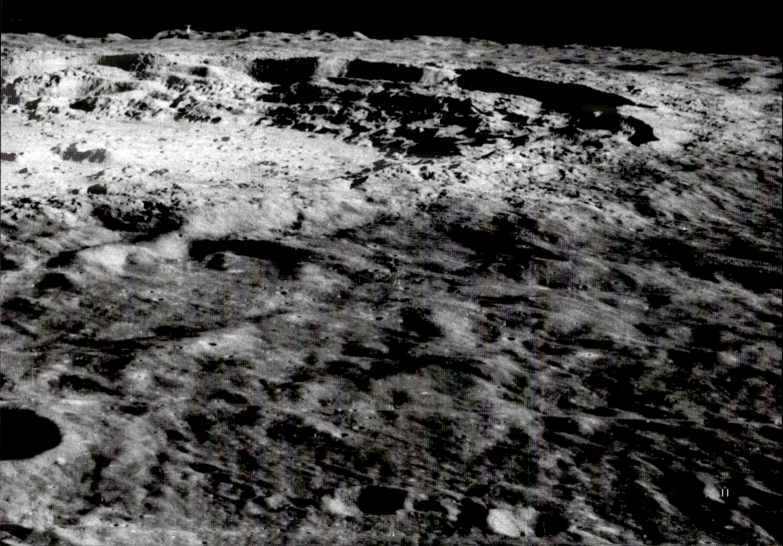

MOONLIGHT

Nothing has fired the human imagination quite like the mysterious Moon. Over the centuries, its gleaming radiance has inspired wonder and worship, pictures and dances, love and loss, fairy tales and horror movies, calendars, rituals and festivals. . . .

⬆ Love and moonlight go hand in hand: *A Carnival Evening* by the French painter Henri Rousseau, 1886.

"And then the moon like to a silver bow new-bent in heaven, shall behold the night of our solemnities."

WILLIAM SHAKESPEARE

LIGHT IN THE DARK

The Moon is our friend. When the world is black and dangerous, it comes to our rescue with its silvery light. You only have to walk down a remote country road under a full Moon to realize why, in ancient times, travelers frequently journeyed by moonlight.

MOON LOVE

Composers, artists, and writers in all places and at all times have taken their inspiration from the silvery disk that fills the world with its eerie beauty. Because it shines at nighttime, the Moon is closely linked to love. Shakespeare's Romeo, the most famous lover of all, swears by the Moon to remain true to Juliet: "Lady, by yonder blesséd moon I vow . . ."

CYCLE OF LIFE

We are moved by the Moon's ceaseless regularity. Day after day, month after month, year after year, it waxes larger, shines at the full, then wanes to a sliver before beginning the sequence again. The pattern reflects the seasons and even life itself.

For thousands of years the Moon was the measure of all time longer than twenty-four hours, and many religious festivals are still fixed by the Moon. But it has its tricks, too. Tradition says that at the full Moon sane people go mad, and men turn into wolves. And this goddess of the night occasionally allows her brilliance to be eclipsed, handing over the world to the powers of darkness and evil.

⬆ John Simmons's *Hermia Surrounded by Fairies* (1861) in *A Midsummer Night's Dream,* standing forlorn in the moonlight.

HOW IT ALL BEGAN

The earliest manned flights were by balloon and airplane: In 1783, Jean-François Pilâtre de Rozier lifted off in a balloon, and over a century later, the Wright brothers flew the first heavier-than-air plane. But balloons and planes were useless for space travel. To go beyond the Earth's atmosphere, a new flying machine was needed.

THE ROCKET

The Chinese invented the rocket over 2,000 years ago. These were simply tubes of bamboo, stuffed with gunpowder (another Chinese invention) and blocked at one end. Starting off as good-fun fireworks, by the fourteenth century rockets were also being used as terrifying weapons.

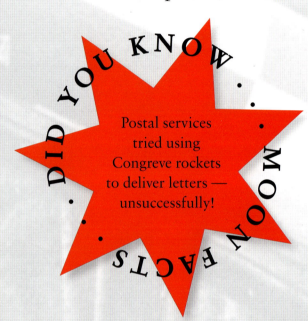

DID YOU KNOW ... MOON FACTS

Postal services tried using Congreve rockets to deliver letters — unsuccessfully!

CONGREVE ROCKETS

Sir William Congreve (1772–1828) advanced rocket science by attaching long guide sticks to his iron-tube missiles, making them fly more accurately. His invention had peaceful as well as military uses: Congreve rockets carrying lines to ships stranded on dangerous rocks saved more than a thousand lives.

⬆ Military missiles: Congreve rockets launched from earthworks, 1827.

LIQUID FUELS

Konstantin Tsiolkovsky (1857–1935) and Robert H. Goddard (1882–1945), both brilliant scientists, pioneered the idea of using rockets for travel beyond the Earth's atmosphere. At the time most people thought their ideas were crazy. The breakthrough was masterminded by Goddard and involved powering a rocket with two liquid fuels: oxygen and kerosene. Although his first liquid-fueled rocket traveled only 184 feet (56 m), it proved that the idea could work.

THE V2

The center of rocket research now shifted to Germany. Here, inspired by the pioneering work of Hermann Oberth (1894–1989), rocket societies were springing up all over the place. In the early 1930s, the German military recognized the potential of rockets as military weapons and appointed the 20-year-old Wernher von Braun (1912–77), one of Oberth's assistants, to lead a high-powered research team.

Von Braun began with an A2 rocket, driven by liquid oxygen and ethanol. This was followed by the experimental A3 and A5 rockets, both used to test mechanisms that he would install in his most famous invention, the A4. This deadly 13-ton (12-tonne) flying bomb, popularly known as the V2, was launched successfully in October 1942.

⬆ A German V2 missile, 1944. Modern space travel developed from the design of this military rocket.

At that moment, the Space Age began. Fired by liquid oxygen and a water-alcohol mix, the massive V2 reached a startling 3,542 mph (5,700 km/h) and could fly a distance of 224 miles (360 km). Far more important as far as the future was concerned, it roared up to an altitude of 54 miles (87 km) — the very edge of space.

"Don't tell me that man doesn't belong out there. Man belongs wherever he wants to go."

WERNHER VON BRAUN

15

ANCIENT EXPLANATIONS

It is easy for most of us, blinded by streetlights and store signs, to forget just how obvious the Moon is in the night sky. Ancient peoples had no such problem. Their Moon was ever present, its movements unchanging. Not surprisingly, they were all fascinated by it.

SUMER SCIENCE

Almost 6,000 years ago, the Sumerians of Mesopotamia (modern Iraq) established the first human civilization. Wondering where the Moon had come from, they came up with the following explanation: Originally, there was just a vast sea or universe. Within this, the heavens and Earth were made, with a solid metal boundary between them. This was in the shape of a vault. Inside this vault floated a sort of gassy atmosphere, some of which was clear and some more solid and bright. The Moon was one of these harder, shiny pieces. This ancient explanation is, in some ways, remarkably close to the latest scientific explanations of how the Moon was formed.

WATERY MOONS

The ancient Chinese had different stories about the Moon's origin. One said there were 12 moons, not one, all of them children of the goddess Heng-O. Each child was made of water and had a hare or a toad living somewhere inside it. These 12 children represented the number of months in a year; during a single year, each new Moon was a different child.

The goddess dwelt at the western end of the heavens. At the start of the month, she washed one of her children — how she washed a water child is not quite clear — before sending it off in a chariot on a month-long journey across the night sky.

↩ Look, no rocket! Heng-O, the Chinese Moon goddess, returns to her silvery kingdom.

⬆ Night prayers: Ancient Egyptian official Sennedjem and his wife, Iyneferty, worship by moonlight.

DID YOU KNOW ... MOON FACTS

A lunar month — a full cycle of the Moon's phases — is actually 29.53059 days!

MOON SACRIFICE

Aztec myth tells how self-sacrifice was needed to keep the Moon alive. When the brave Conch Shell Lord surrendered his life to keep the night light shining, he was mysteriously reborn as the Moon itself.

TOWARD SCIENCE

All early civilizations explained the Moon in terms of myth and religion. Then, around 2,500 years ago, a group of brilliant Greek philosophers began to challenge such unscientific ideas.

A Roman mosaic of the Greek philosopher Anaximander, the first person to hint at a boundless universe.

THE IONIANS

The thinkers who questioned traditional teachings are sometimes said to belong to the "Ionian School" of philosophy. This does not mean that they went to a single school or even university; rather, most came from the Ionian part of the Greek world (western Turkey), centered around the port of Miletus.

Although the Ionian philosophers had widely differing ideas, they all agreed on one key position: The way to understand all things, including the nature of the Moon, was through reason, not myth or religion. Anaximander, for instance, said that all matter, from the Moon to mildew, was made of the same basic substance. We might agree, calling that substance atoms, or protons, neutrons, and electrons.

"The Sun, the Moon, and all the stars are stones of fire, which are carried round by the revolution of the aether [the heavens]."

GREEK PHILOSOPHER ANAXAGORAS

ANAXAGORAS

Around 464 BCE, the philosopher Anaxagoras brought Ionian ideas to Athens, the most important city in the Greek world. The Moon's light, he taught correctly, is not its own but comes from the Sun. The Sun, he noted, is a red-hot stone that can be eclipsed when the Moon passes in front of it.

This was all too radical for the average Athenian. Anaxagoras was punished for his ideas and banished from the city. The man we might call the "Father of Modern Science" returned to Ionia, where he continued to work until his death in 428 BCE. Many centuries would pass before his thoughts about the Moon were proved correct.

SEVEN DAYS A WEEK

The idea of a week being made up of seven days has two origins. (1) The Moon has roughly four phases, each with seven days; (2) seven was a sacred number for the Jews.

➔ The hammer-shaped symbol for Hebrew's sacred number 7.

↙ A ruined temple in Ionia, the home province of some of the most advanced thinkers of the ancient world.

INTO ORBIT!

After the Second World War, there was great rivalry between the USA and the USSR (Soviet Union). The Communist Soviets believed the Americans wanted to destroy the Soviet system of government; for their part, the Americans were afraid that the Soviets were trying to spread Communism around the world.

THE COLD WAR

These two superpowers — America and the Soviet Union — never actually fought each other, but they vigorously prepared for war. This resulted in a period known as the "Cold War," in which each country built up huge supplies of weapons and invented new ones. Horrifyingly dangerous though all this was, it greatly helped the development of space technology.

World War II had seen the development of missiles and nuclear weapons. The next step, argued the army generals, was to combine the two into an intercontinental ballistic missile (ICBM) carrying a nuclear warhead. The aim was to build V2-like missiles capable of flying thousands of miles from one continent to another.

Other military experts were calling for "spy satellites": man-made devices circling the Earth and taking pictures of enemy territory from space. The competition to produce the first ICBMs and satellites sped up research so much that by 1957 the media was talking of an American–Soviet "Space Race."

VON BRAUN

By the end of World War II, rocket scientist von Braun and his German team were already planning a rocket capable of crossing the Atlantic Ocean. These men were taken to the United States and invited to continue their research. Working for the US Army, they produced a super-V2 missile called the *Redstone* and made the first two-stage rocket by placing a small Corporal missile on top of an old V2.

What really interested von Braun, however, was not missiles, but space rockets. For the time being, though, he was unable to pursue this line of development because the Americans put military needs first. Then, on October 4, 1957, they received a nasty shock.

⬆ German rocket genius Wernher von Braun (right) explains his *Redstone* rocket to a US Army expert.

⬆ Ready to go! A Soviet technician makes a few final adjustments to *Sputnik*, the first man-made satellite.

SPUTNIK

Unknown to the Americans, a team of Soviet scientists led by Sergey Korolyov (1907–66) had already designed, built, and tested a gigantic two-stage ICBM, called the R-7. Once they knew it worked, the Soviets decided to announce it to the world in the most striking way possible. Working night and day, Soviet scientists made a small satellite fitted with two radio transmitters. Its name was *Sputnik*, meaning "fellow traveler." A modified R-7 launched it into orbit around Earth, and fascinated millions listened to *Sputnik*'s mesmerizing beep-beep signals.

The Space Race had truly begun.

DID YOU KNOW . . . MOON FACTS

The first US satellite launch failed: The *Vanguard* rocket blew up seconds after liftoff!

21

WHAT'S IN A NAME?

Many modern words for the Moon originated with the Sumerians of ancient Mesopotamia. They called the full Moon *Nanna* and the crescent Moon *Sin*. From *Sin* came the ancient Greek word for the Moon, *Selene*. This changed over time to make the modern *lune* (French), *luna* (Italian), and many others.

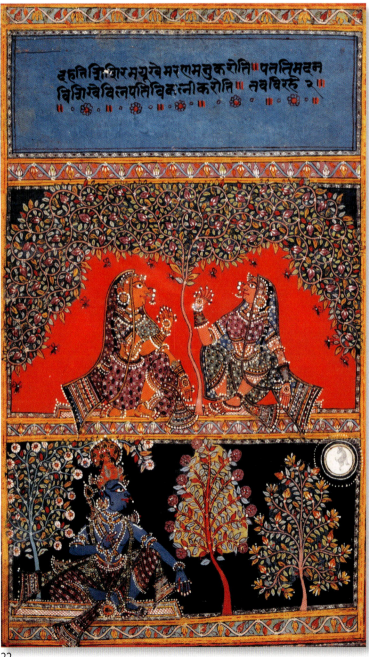

MOON MEASURES

Another group of languages, including Dutch, Swedish, English, and German, all have a word for "Moon" that begins with an "M." These Moon words have nothing at all to do with *Sin*. Instead, they are related to the word "month." Most scholars believe all of them began with the really ancient word *me*. This meant "to measure."

What does "Moon" have to do with measuring? The answer is not too difficult to figure out: In nearly all ancient civilizations, the Moon was the measure of time. A full cycle of its phases, waxing and waning, made up a month. In other words, the Moon got its name because it was a sort of gigantic heavenly clock!

The old Asian language Sanskrit has many words for the Moon. Two of them are *kalavat* and *kalanidhi*. These also remind us of the Moon's usefulness for keeping track of time: from the Sanskrit comes our word "calendar" — something that measures out days and months.

◐ "Burned by the cold light of the Moon": an illustration from a Sanskrit manuscript.

ONE AND MANY

Many languages and cultures have similar names for the Moon at different times of the year. These are linked to what was going on at the time. In the lands of the Northern Hemisphere, for instance, there is nearly always a late summer "Harvest Moon" and a wintry "Cold Moon" or "Snow Moon." More frightening still was the howling "Wolf Moon."

DID YOU KNOW . . .

MOON FACTS

The Muslim name for God — Allah — may have come from an ancient Moon god.

⊕ The Harvest Moon — the full Moon nearest the autumnal equinox — was so called because wise farmers had to have their harvest safely gathered by then.

CULTURAL DIFFERENCES

Past cultures had poetic names for their Moon months. Hungry North American Choctaw Indians spoke of March's "Big Famine Moon." The Celts had a "Singing Moon" (September), while October was China's "Kindly Moon."

SPACEMEN

By 1960, Soviet and American scientists were racing to get a person into space. They started with a dog, then tried monkeys, and finally, using even bigger rockets, launched men and women into orbit. Peering out of their cramped capsules, they became the first human beings to gaze down in wonder at the green-blue sphere we call Earth.

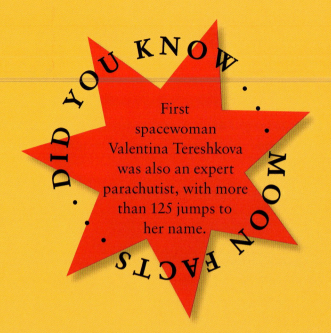

DID YOU KNOW . . . MOON FACTS

First spacewoman Valentina Tereshkova was also an expert parachutist, with more than 125 jumps to her name.

ANIMALS

Using the same type of rocket as *Sputnik I*, in November 1957 the Soviets launched *Sputnik II* with "an experimental animal" — the hunting dog Laika — on board. Official statements said she died peacefully after circling the Earth.

Gordo, the American bushy-tailed monkey, survived his 15-minute flight, but drowned when his mini capsule sank in the ocean. Later US space monkeys survived, as did a number of Soviet dogs. The time had now come to try a human being.

GAGARIN

On April 12, 1961, the twenty-seven-year-old Soviet cosmonaut Major Yuri Gagarin was strapped into the "Swallow" capsule atop a huge *Vostok* rocket and blasted into orbit around the Earth. After an historic journey of 108 minutes, the world's first spaceman safely reentered the atmosphere and

⊙ Chimpanzee Ham is welcomed on board the US recovery ship after his space flight in a *Redstone* rocket. Laika the space dog (above).

parachuted to the ground — and instant celebrity.

The first American in space, Alan Shepard, made his journey on May 5, 1961. After this, the pace quickened. In August, a Soviet cosmonaut spent a whole day in space. The following February, American John Glenn made three Earth orbits. Valentina Tereshkova became the first spacewoman in June 1963. Meanwhile, US President John F. Kennedy had made his famous pledge to put a man on the Moon by the end of the decade.

YURI GAGARIN

Born in a small Russian village, Yuri Gagarin (1934-68) trained in secret for two years before becoming the world's first spaceman. He was made a Hero of the Soviet Union and enjoyed worldwide fame before dying in a flying accident.

The first batch of Americans to train as astronauts.

25

MUSLIM FOUNDATIONS

During the Middle Ages, most Europeans accepted the view of the Universe outlined by the Greek philosopher Ptolemy in about 150 CE. This had the Earth at its center, with the Sun, Moon, and stars circling around it in crystal spheres. More accurate scientific thought developed farther east, in the Muslim world.

WHY ISLAM?

The *Koran*, the holy book of Islam, encouraged believers to think of the heavens as being governed by God's laws. Working out how heavenly bodies moved, therefore, was a way of learning more about God. This encouraged a scientific way of thinking: making observations, then working out laws that fitted them. Muslim scientists studied the Moon especially carefully because their calendar, with its holy months, was Moon-based.

Medieval Islam was quite tolerant toward other faiths and had no problem accepting the scientific ideas of non-Muslims. This allowed them to borrow from Indian scholars, for example. Furthermore, the great Islamic centers of learning — Baghdad and Damascus — were in the center of the educated world. Scholars, books, and ideas could easily get there from Greece, Persia, and India.

⬤ A 19th-century view of the Syrian city of Damascus, a famous city of Islamic scholarship in the early Middle Ages.

THE ISLAMIC GOLDEN AGE

Between the eighth and thirteenth centuries, Islamic scholarship enjoyed a Golden Age. Brilliant scientists like al-Biruni, al-Sijzi, and ibn-Rushd (also known as Averroës) laid the foundations for Europe's Scientific Revolution.

By careful observation, astronomers worked out that the Earth and Moon went around the Sun, that the planets' orbits were not neat circles but ellipses, that the Moon was lit by the Sun's light, and that the Earth spun. They also considered the force of gravity, centuries before the more famous work of Sir Isaac Newton.

PTOLEMY

Working in Alexandria, Egypt, the great scholar Ptolemy (c. 100–165 CE) set out in several books everything known about the Earth and the heavens. Unfortunately, a lot of it was wrong!

NEW MOON

In the Western world, a lunar month began with a new Moon. A new Islamic month began at a different point: when, looking west, the crescent Moon first became visible in the evening sky.

➲ Pondering Moon mysteries: a statue of the remarkable Spanish-Arab scholar ibn-Rushd, commonly known in Europe as Averroës.

MOON GODS

Ancient peoples gazing up at the moon were awestruck. What was the glorious object that filled the night sky, that glided across the heavens, waxing and waning with perfect regularity? There could be only one answer: It was a god.

MR. MOON

Most cultures outside ancient Greece and Rome thought of the Moon as masculine: We talk of a "Man in the Moon," for example, and the Germans of *Herr Mond*, "Mister Moon." As a god, he was commonly seen as the male side of a pairing with a female Sun goddess. In such cases, the Sun was feminine, probably because she made things grow.

In the Japanese Shinto religion, the Moon god, Tsuki-Yomi, was born from the right eye of Izanagi, the first god, while the Sun goddess, Amaterasu, came from his left eye. At first, brother and sister got along well and traveled through the sky together. But after Tsuki-Yomi killed the food goddess because she made him a foul-looking meal from her mouth and nose, Amaterasu disowned her brother. From that time on, the Sun and Moon never shared the same sky.

SKY CHASE

The Inuit people also had a Moon god, Anningan, who did not get along with his sister, the Sun goddess, Malina. He disliked her so much that he chased her across the sky, day after day. Obsessed with the chase, he forgot to eat. That is how the Inuit explained the Moon getting smaller and smaller before Anningan stopped to eat and got bigger again!

Soma, the Hindu Moon god, rode on a chariot pulled by beautiful white steeds. His Moon contained a magic liquid that gave eternal life to all who drank it. When the gods were guzzling Soma's potion to maintain their immortality, he waned to just an empty sliver.

DID YOU KNOW... MOON FACTS

Thoth is often shown as an ibis. The bird's long, curved beak represents the crescent Moon.

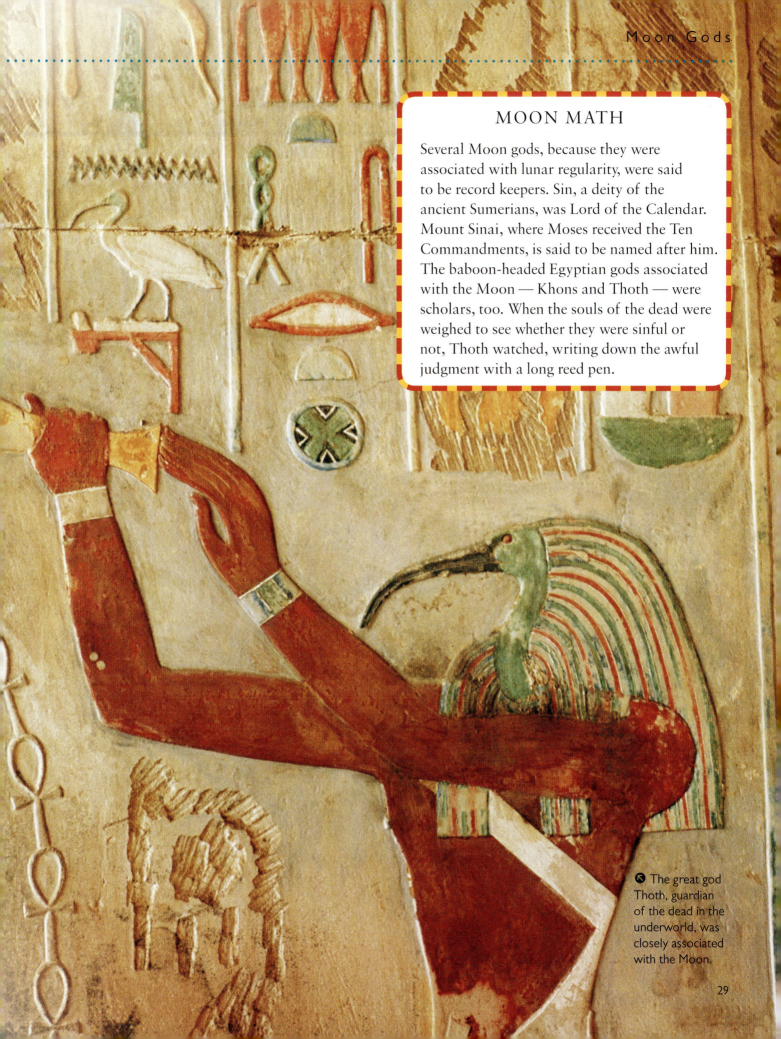

MOON MATH

Several Moon gods, because they were associated with lunar regularity, were said to be record keepers. Sin, a deity of the ancient Sumerians, was Lord of the Calendar. Mount Sinai, where Moses received the Ten Commandments, is said to be named after him. The baboon-headed Egyptian gods associated with the Moon — Khons and Thoth — were scholars, too. When the souls of the dead were weighed to see whether they were sinful or not, Thoth watched, writing down the awful judgment with a long reed pen.

The great god Thoth, guardian of the dead in the underworld, was closely associated with the Moon.

29

MOON GODDESSES

The ancient Greeks and Romans thought of the Moon as female. Modern Latin-based languages also make the noun "Moon" feminine: the French *la lune*, for example. The Moon remains a lady, too, in the eyes of American and European poets.

⬆ Love by moonlight: The Moon goddess, Selene, gazes longingly at the beautiful shepherd Endymion.

SELENE

The beautiful Selene was a daughter of two giant Titans and a sister of the Sun and of the Dawn. According to Greek mythology, she fell in love with the unbelievably handsome shepherd Endymion. To ensure he never left her, she persuaded Zeus, the King of the Gods, to send the youth to sleep forever in a cave on Mount Latmus. The Romans knew Selene as Luna.

THE DARK SIDE

Hecate, the goddess of the not-yet-risen Moon, was altogether less pleasant than Selene. Her realm was witchcraft, ghosts, and ghouls, and she dwelt on tombs, at crossroads, and where the blood of murder victims fell.

The Aztec goddess Coyolxauhqui was another Moon deity associated with grim events. When she argued with her mother, her furious newborn brother viciously killed her and her 400 other brothers and sisters. In a gesture of savage kindness, he chopped Coyolxauhqui up and threw her head into the sky so her mother could still see her — in the form of the Moon.

DID YOU KNOW . . . MOON FACTS

In later times, the Romans replaced the Moon goddess Luna with Diana, the hunting virgin.

⤴ The Queen of Ghosts and triple-headed ruler of a dark and moonless world, Hecate had originally been a far more comforting mother figure.

MOON WORSHIP

Ancient peoples were in awe of the Moon. For a start, it was mysteriously beautiful. It was obviously powerful too, as anyone living by the sea noticed: The highest tides coincided with the fullest Moon. The Moon's regular changes also gave pattern to life. Clearly, it was something to be worshipped.

⬆ The Pyramid of the Moon, built for the worship of the Moon goddess, Chalchiutlicue, in the pre-Aztec city of Teotihuacan.

STONEHENGE

The 5,000-year-old monument known as Stonehenge in England was perhaps a gigantic calculator. The circles and rectangles, marked with stones and ditches, allowed the priests to predict eclipses of the Sun and Moon over hundreds of years.

SACRIFICE

Worship means recognizing in public that something or someone is tremendously powerful and needs to be kept on your side. How do you make the Moon god or goddess happy? The Egyptians did it by fashioning a statue of the god and offering it food every day. Other primitive religions had images of the Moon carved in stone or wood.

Ancient Hindu ritual involved offering sacrifices to the Moon — demonstrating its importance by giving it the most precious things worshippers possessed: food, an animal, or even a human life. The Aztecs' ritual of cutting out human hearts was associated with sacrifice to the Moon goddess, Coyolxauhqui.

LIGHT AND SHADE

Moon worship changed with the phases. Full Moon was a time of bright light and joy, when worshippers danced, sang, and took part in rituals. Some African mothers washed their newborn babies by moonlight to make them especially pure.

The three days in each month when there is no Moon were the opposite: nights of absolute darkness, when the powers of evil threatened to take over the world. Some peoples saw this as a time of battle, when the silvery moon was being attacked. To help it fight off its opponent and return to light the Earth, worshippers made loud noises to scare off the Moon's enemy.

"Whenever you have need of anything, once in a month . . . when the Moon is full, ye shall assemble in some secret place and adore the spirit of Me who am Queen of all Witches."

A MODERN MOON-WORSHIP RITUAL

You would laugh too, if you had seen, What the Moon saw, on HALLOWE'EN.

⬆ Postcard witches dance by the light of a smiling Moon.

SCIENCE'S REVOLUTION

The Scientific Revolution swept Europe in the sixteenth and seventeenth centuries. It completely changed how scientists worked. Previously, they had fitted the facts to suit a theory. Now they started with observations and found a theory that explained them. Several Islamic scholars had done this from the ninth to eleventh centuries, but their work had not been explored.

COPERNICUS

In *On the Revolutions of the Heavenly Spheres* (1543), the scholar Copernicus (1473–1543) set out three world-changing theories: (1) the planets of the Solar System revolve around the Sun; (2) the planet Earth goes around the Sun once a year; (3) the Earth spins, making one complete rotation each day. These ideas overturned what European scholars had believed for many centuries.

ALL CHANGE

The Polish scientist Mikolaj Kopernik, known in English as Nicolaus Copernicus, is recognized as the father of modern astronomy. He traveled all over Europe, studying many subjects before making a name for himself as an astronomer. Besides being a scholar, he worked as a military governor, judge, doctor, and tax collector!

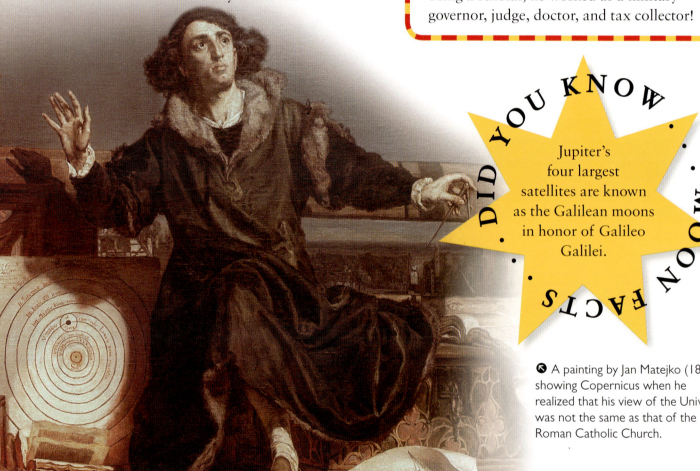

DID YOU KNOW . MOON FACTS

Jupiter's four largest satellites are known as the Galilean moons in honor of Galileo Galilei.

A painting by Jan Matejko (1872) showing Copernicus when he realized that his view of the Universe was not the same as that of the Roman Catholic Church.

↑ You're wrong! Cristiano Banti's painting (1857) of priests telling Galileo to change his views about the Universe.

LOOKING AT THE MOON

Copernicus's ideas were all very good, but he could not prove them, so they remained theoretical. It was left to others to test them with evidence. The Danish scientist Tycho Brahe (1546–1601) came up with many observations that supported the Polish genius.

Englishman William Gilbert (1544–1603) described the Earth as a "great magnet," which helped the German mathematician Johannes Kepler (1571–1630) propose laws explaining a living, moving universe.

GALILEO

Galileo Galilei (1564–1642) was an Italian scientist. He claimed that mathematics, not Bible study, was needed to understand the Universe. Using his telescope, he was the first person to study the Moon in detail, noting its mountains and craters.

Galileo's telescope also showed that Jupiter had moons of its own, a discovery that demanded a whole new way of looking at the Solar System. The Earth was no longer at the center of creation, nor was its moon unique. Where in the heavens, people asked, was all this new thinking leading?

MOON PROBES

During the early 1960s, Soviet and American programs prepared for an eventual Moon mission. Key things to work on were detailed knowledge of the lunar surface, getting safely back into the Earth's atmosphere, and living in a zero-gravity environment.

⬆ Planets, stars, and space travel: the NASA logo of 1969. It was known jokingly as the "meatball"!

At first, the Soviet Union focused its energies on the Space Race more efficiently than the United States. In response to this, in 1958, the Americans set up NASA (National Aeronautics and Space Administration), which gradually brought together the military, civilian, and business sides of the space program. By the mid-1960s, the United States was starting to pull ahead of its rival.

SOVIET SHOTS

Two years before Yuri Gagarin (1934–68) became the first person to circle the Earth, the Soviet *Luna 1* had made the 238,855-mile (384,400 km) journey to the Moon, passing only 3,728 miles (6,000 km) from its barren surface. A few months later, *Luna 2* actually crashed into the Moon and *Luna 3* flew right around it, taking pictures of the "dark side," which humans had never previously seen. Finally, in 1966, *Luna 9* became the first craft to make a soft landing on the Moon's surface.

Meanwhile, Soviet cosmonauts were learning how to live in space. In 1964, *Voskhod* ("Sunrise") *1* saw three men launched into space at the same time — the world's first multiperson mission. A year later, Alexei Leonov (b. 1934) became the first space walker when he opened an airlock and ventured outside *Voskhod 2*.

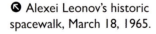

⊘ Alexei Leonov's historic spacewalk, March 18, 1965.

BAD LANDING

Alexei Leonov's pioneering spacewalk was less dangerous than what awaited him back on Earth. When his craft missed its landing ground and came down in thick forest, he and his fellow cosmonaut had to fend off savage wolves before they were rescued!

RANGERS AND SURVEYORS

The aim of the American unmanned *Ranger* program was to take close-up photographs of the lunar surface. It made a disastrous start when *Ranger 1* to 6 either failed to take off, missed their target, or malfunctioned. In the end, though, *Ranger 7* to 9 (1964–65) managed to take the pictures NASA wanted.

These missions paved the way for the unmanned *Surveyor* flights. Two crashed on the Moon's surface, but the other five came down safely. More significantly, *Surveyor* 6 managed to take off again. Before long, US astronauts were walking in space and linking up ("docking") two orbiting spacecraft. The pieces were coming together for the greatest mission of all: the *Apollo* program to land human beings on the Moon.

◐ Preparing the way: *Surveyor I* takes off on a mission to find a safe landing spot on the Moon, June 1966.

APOLLO — THE TRAGEDY

The launch of *Sputnik* and Gagarin's space flight showed the world that the Soviet Union led the United States in the Space Race. What could the Americans do to get back that lead? What "first" could they achieve? US President John F. Kennedy turned to von Braun for the answers. The pioneer of modern rocketry replied that the United States' best hope was to land a man on the Moon before the Soviets. Kennedy took up the challenge.

MODULES

It was all very good talking about going to the Moon, but how was it to be achieved? A number of key questions had to be answered. The first was whether the voyage would be made in a single flight, or from a space station built after many flights. The one-flight option was chosen because it was cheaper.

The scientists then had to decide the best way of getting astronauts down onto the lunar surface. They opted for a three-module scheme: A service module (SM) with powerful engines would contain supplies; a command module (CM) would house the astronauts on their way to and from the Moon; and a lunar module (LM) would actually land there. Joined together, all three would be launched toward their destination by a mighty rocket.

➡ The three modules of the *Apollo* lunar craft.

Service module

Rocket motor

Launch escape system

Command module

Lunar module

"I believe that this nation should commit itself to achieving the goal, before this decade is out, of landing a man on the Moon and returning him safely to the Earth."

PRESIDENT JOHN F. KENNEDY, 1961

⬆ *Apollo*'s astronauts from left: Gus Grissom, Ed White, and Roger Chaffee died when fire broke out in their *Apollo 1* command module during training.

TRAGEDY

Every stage of the journey and every piece of equipment had to be tested and retested to make sure it functioned perfectly. The *Gemini* missions, for example, tested the docking of two craft in space. This was vital because *Apollo*'s command module

⬆ The *Apollo 1* command module after the fatal fire.

and lunar module needed to separate and come together again.

Disaster struck on the very first mission. *Apollo 1* was to test the combined service and command modules in space. On January 27, before the rocket even lifted off, a fire broke ou in the command module during a testing sessi The three astronauts on board were burned to death. At that moment, the Moon seemed far

DID YOU KNOW...

NASA's Dr. Abe Silverstein named the *Apollo* mission after the Greek god who rode a chariot across the skies.

...MOON

NEWTON'S MOON

By the late seventeenth century, scientific understanding of the Moon had come a long way. The ancient Greeks, the Muslim scholars of the Middle Ages, Kepler, and Galileo had all played their parts. The stage was now set for Sir Isaac Newton to put in place key pieces of the great jigsaw puzzle.

UNIVERSAL GENIUS

The Englishman Sir Isaac Newton (1642–1727) was a scientist and mathematician of rare genius. His work covered many fields. He invented calculus — a way of working with numbers that are continually changing — and he discovered that white light is made up of a spectrum of all the colors. Far more important, where the Moon was concerned, was his work with gravity.

The apple legend: a fanciful image of Isaac Newton wondering what makes the apple fall. Such pondering produced his theory of gravity.

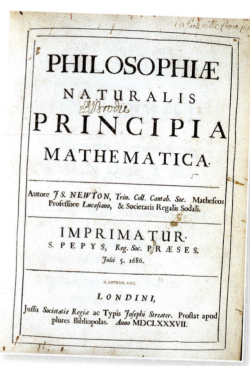

Newton's *Principia Mathematica* (1687) outlined a universe interpreted through mathematics.

WEIGHT AND SEE

Newton described a force that attracts every single particle in the Universe to every other particle. He called it "gravity," from the Latin *gravitas*, meaning "weight." He also said it was possible to work out the gravitational attraction between objects. This law of gravity, he explained, depends on (a) the mass of objects and (b) how far apart they are.

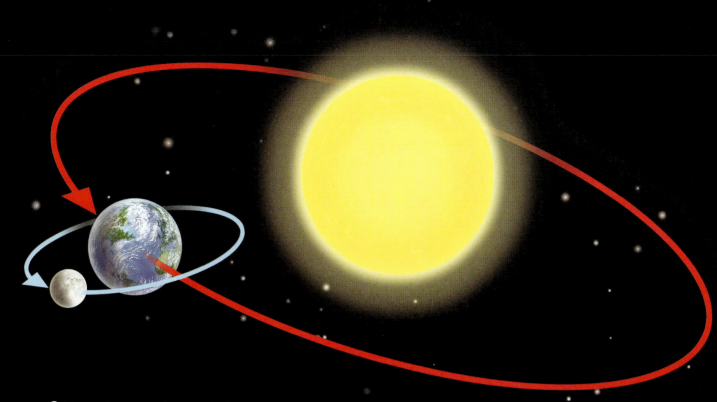

⬆ Newton's theory of gravity finally explained the orbit of the Moon around the Earth.

"If I have been able to see further, it was only because I stood on the shoulders of giants."

SIR ISAAC NEWTON, IN A LETTER TO FELLOW SCIENTIST ROBERT HOOKE

APPLES AND PLANETS

By Newton's time, it was known that the planets went around the Sun and the Moon went around the Earth. But no one had been able to explain their paths, which are ellipses rather than neat circles. Newton's theory of gravity was the missing link.

Using complex mathematics, Newton showed that the force making an apple fall from a tree is precisely the same as that keeping the Moon in orbit around the Earth. Suddenly, the Moon's path made sense: It is attracted by both the Earth's gravity and the Sun's, the latter pulling it into an ellipse. The gravitational pull of the Moon also explained the rise and fall of the tides. At last, the Universe was beginning to make scientific sense.

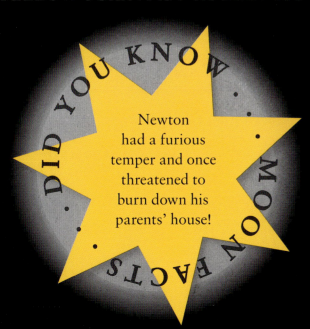

DID YOU KNOW ... MOON FACTS

Newton had a furious temper and once threatened to burn down his parents' house!

41

HEY DIDDLE DIDDLE!

From nursery rhymes to good luck charms, Moon myths are deeply embedded in the traditional culture of every land. A full Moon was thought to bring good fortune, so those born under one enjoyed lucky lives. Similarly, for centuries, wise Scottish women refused to marry unless the Moon was full.

BLUE MOON

Because the solar and lunar calendars are slightly different, occasionally a year has 13 full Moons instead of 12. The rare thirteenth is a "blue" Moon, giving us the expression "once in a blue Moon."

"Hey diddle diddle,
The cat and the fiddle,
The cow jumped over
the Moon.
The little dog laughed
to see such fun,
And the dish ran away
with the spoon."

◗ Arthur Rackham's weirdly fascinating illustration of "Hey Diddle Diddle."

JUST A DITTY?

The Cat and Fiddle nursery rhyme, with its silly words and catchy sounds, has been beloved of children for generations. But is that all it is, just jolly nonsense? Some scholars believe it was written to mock Queen Elizabeth I. She was the "cow" who was in love ("over the Moon") with Robert Dudley, Earl of Leicester — the "dog"!

Another idea is that the names — cat, fiddle, cow, little dog, Moon, dish, spoon — were features of the night sky. The Moon is obvious, while the cat, for example, was the constellation Leo, the lion. When they all appeared at the same time, in April, it was time to sow crops. So what we consider a children's rhyme might really have been a piece of advice to farmers.

BOYS AND GIRLS . . . !

Among the many, many children's rhymes mentioning the Moon, the English language also has:

*"Boys and girls, come out to play.
The Moon doth shine as bright as day."*

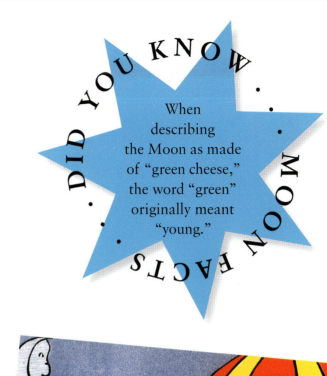

DID YOU KNOW . . . MOON FACTS

When describing the Moon as made of "green cheese," the word "green" originally meant "young."

❷ I see the Moon: an illustration for Edward Lear's limerick about a man who "built a balloon to examine the Moon."

*"I see the Moon
and the Moon sees me —
The Moon sees the somebody
I'd like to see."*

TRADITIONAL CHILDREN'S
RHYME

MAN IN THE MOON

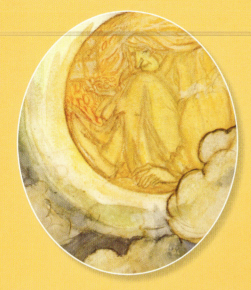

Gaze up at the full Moon on a clear night and — yes! — it has a face. Since ancient times, people looking upon those mysterious features have been inspired to dream and tell stories. Here are two of them. . . .

⬆ Can you see him? Florence Harrison's *Man in the Moon* (1918).

THE WISE FROG *(An Angolan tale)*

The mighty King of the Earth decided that his beloved son would only marry a daughter of the King of the Moon. No one but the Wise Frog knew how to deliver the proposal: When the Moon King's daughters came down to Earth to drink, he hid in one of their water buckets and was carried home with them. Safe on the Moon, he delivered his master's invitation.

The Moon King was delighted and sent a letter of acceptance back to Earth with the frog, who was rewarded with juicy pork and chicken. Two days later, the Moon Princess descended to Earth on a thread woven by the magical Moon Spider, and the wedding took place amid great feasting and merriment.

⬈ Chasing the light: Wolves Skoll (Repulsion) and Hati (Hate) pursue the Sun and Moon across the skies. If they are caught, the world will be plunged into freezing darkness. (*Ancient Norse myth*)

HYUKI AND BIL *(A German tale)*

One night, at their father's request, the fair children Hyuki and Bil climbed a sacred hill to draw the enchanted liquor, song mead, from a magical spring that flowed there. They filled their wooden bucket to the brim, hoisted it to their shoulders on a pole, and, with mead spilling onto the dewy grass, began to make their way down the hill again.

At that moment, Mani, the handsome son of the great god Odin, swooped down in his Moon chariot and carried off Hyuki and Bil to his eerie kingdom. And that is where they remain, their shadows making the dark spots on the face of the Moon.

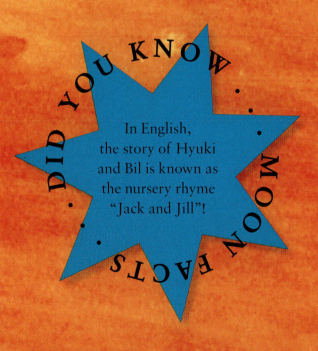

. . . DID YOU KNOW . . . MOON FACTS . . .

In English, the story of Hyuki and Bil is known as the nursery rhyme "Jack and Jill"!

CREATION

We saw on page 11 how scientists now believe the Moon was created by a gigantic interplanetary impact. This idea (number one below) remains just one of several theories, however. Three other ideas all have their supporters.

THEORY ONE: IMPACT

Four and a half billion years ago, a passing body about the size of Mars slapped into the cooling Earth. The rocky particles arising from the collision formed a ring around the Earth that eventually combined to form the Moon. This is currently the most widely accepted theory.

THEORY TWO: FISSION

After its creation, the gassy-fluid Earth-to-be was spinning at great speed. The velocity was so great that a huge lump of Earth matter was flung off and solidified into the Moon. Modern scientists are unhappy with the flinging-off part of this notion — they just don't believe it could have happened.

THEORY THREE: CO-ACCRETION

When the Solar System was forming, a cloud of spinning gas and dust grew more and more dense. At some stage, it split in two. These lumps solidified into the Earth and Moon— meaning the two bodies share the same swirling parent cloud. This idea does not explain the movements of the bodies in the present Solar System.

THEORY FOUR: CAPTURE

Having been formed somewhere else in the Universe, the Moon soared through space for millions — perhaps billions — of years. Eventually, it entered our Solar System on a course close to the Earth. Our gravity was powerful enough to slow the zooming Moon and hold it in an Earthly orbit, which is where it has been ever since.

⬆ Galactic mystery: creation in action in the distant Universe.

⬆ Simpler explanation: a medieval Bible illustration of God creating the Moon, on the fourth day of the creation of the world.

METAL AND MANTLE

The "impact" theory of Moon creation is supported by its relative lack of iron. This could be because it was formed from debris smashed off the Earth's mantle (outer layer), not its iron-rich inner core.

MOON MEN!

We sailed west until we came across a remote island with a wine-filled river. . . . Refreshed, we set out again only for a gigantic waterspout to lift our boat to the Moon. . . .

Thus begins the world's first sci-fi tale: *True Story* (*c.* 165 CE) by the Greek writer Lucian.

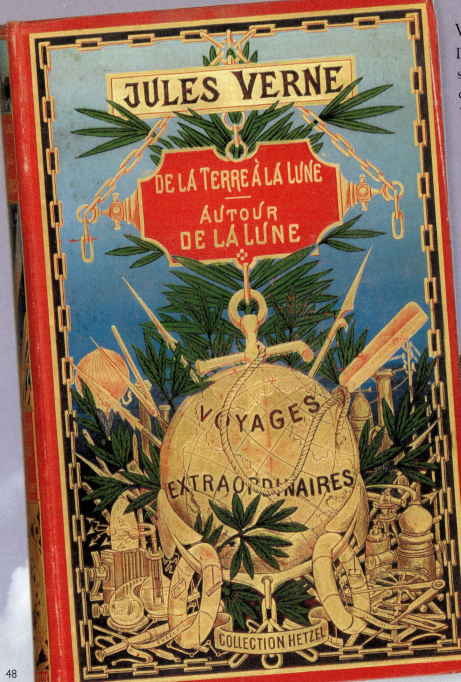

VERNE AND WELLS

Despite Lucian and a few others, science fiction did not really catch on until the nineteenth century. The first modern writer to pen a popular Moon story was the Frenchman Jules Verne. *From the Earth to the Moon* (originally *De la Terre à la Lune*, 1865) tells of three men building a gigantic cannon that will shoot them to the Moon. It works, and Verne finishes the story in *Around the Moon* (1870): The astronauts fall back to Earth at 257,683 mph (414,700 km/h) — and survive!

◖ Sci-fi is born: the French edition of Jules Verne's *From the Earth to the Moon* and *Around the Moon*.

Verne's space travelers find the Moon uninhabited. Not so with the pair of heroes of H. G. Wells's *The First Men in the Moon* (1901). Their Moon is inhabited by tiny, humanlike creatures called Selenites, who live underground. The Wells spaceship, made weightless by gravity-defying "cavorite," is powered by air pressure.

ENDLESS INSPIRATION

By the 1950s, dozens of science fiction stories about the Moon were being published every year. The comic hero Tintin went there in 1954. In the same year, one of the most famous science fiction writers of all, Arthur C. Clarke, published *Prelude to Space*, the first of his many Moon stories.

Since then, the flood of Moon stories has been unstoppable. They feature nuclear rockets, Moon mining, Moon colonies, Moon life, parallel Moon universes. . . . The power of our silvery neighbor to fire the human imagination knows no limits.

➲ Intellectual problem: Claude Shepperson's impression of Moon-dwelling Selenite workers carrying a thinker who is incapable of walking because of his oversized brain!

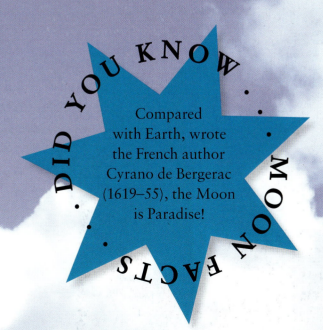

DID YOU KNOW . . . MOON FACTS

Compared with Earth, wrote the French author Cyrano de Bergerac (1619–55), the Moon is Paradise!

THE MIGHTY *SATURN*

The journey to the Moon required a rocket larger than anything yet devised. Fortunately, von Braun (see page 15) had already begun such a machine. Named after the planet Saturn, it was based upon his designs for a missile able to bombard the USA from Germany.

EARTHSHAKING

The *Saturn V* rocket was one of the most awesome machines ever built. It stood as tall as St. Paul's Cathedral in London, 363 feet (111 m), and was broader than the center circle of a full-size soccer field, 32.8 feet (10 m). When full of fuel, it weighed a gigantic 3,307 tons (3,000 tonnes) — five times the weight of the largest aircraft ever built.

Getting this monster off the ground required stupendous force. Von Braun provided this not with a single engine but with five bundled together like sticks of dynamite. The force they created was a hundred times greater than that used to lift astronaut Alan Shepard into space on May 5, 1961.

⬆ The brilliant German rocket scientist Wernher von Braun. In the background is his largest creation, the mammoth *Saturn V*.

THREE STAGES

To get into orbit 112 miles (180 km) around the Earth, a rocket needs to reach 17,398 mph (28,000 km/h). It must then accelerate to nearly 24,855 mph (40,000 km/h) to escape Earth's gravity. Such speeds mean burning vast quantities of fuel. In just the first 2.5 minutes of its journey, the *Saturn V* consumed 4.5 million pounds (2 million kg) of fuel. This left the problem of a huge empty tank to haul along.

Von Braun solved this issue by splitting his rocket into three stages. The first stage, powered by a special rocket fuel and liquid oxygen, lifted *Saturn V* 38 miles (61 km) above the Earth and pushed it to a speed of 5,344 mph (8,600 km/h). That stage then fell away, dropping into the Atlantic Ocean, and Stage 2, fueled by liquid hydrogen and oxygen, took over. This drove the rocket to near escape velocity (the speed at which the craft could escape the Earth's gravity) at a height of 115 miles (185 km). When that stage also burned out, Stage 3 flung *Apollo* and its astronauts toward the distant Moon.

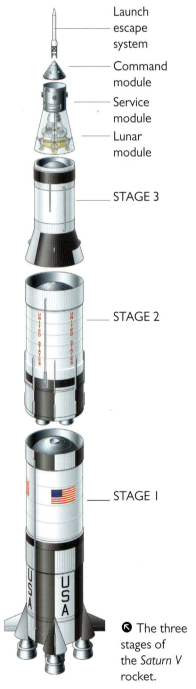

Launch escape system

Command module

Service module

Lunar module

STAGE 3

STAGE 2

STAGE 1

◗ The three stages of the *Saturn V* rocket.

When the engines of the *Saturn V* rocket were tested, the earth quivered 50 miles (80 km) away.

⬈ Reaching for the skies: *Saturn V*, the fifth version of the rocket of that name, being prepared for takeoff in the specially built Vertical Assembly Building.

BIG ROCKET — BIG HOUSE

To house the *Saturn V* rocket, NASA had to construct the world's largest single-story building. At 525 feet (160 m) tall and covering 8 acres (3.24 hectares), the Vertical Assembly Building (VAB) is so huge that it has its own weather: Rain clouds form below the roof.

MOON MOVIES

The movie industry loves the idea and image of the Moon. In 2007 alone, for instance, it released films entitled *Moon*, *MoonBaseOne*, *Moon To*, *Half Moon*, *Under the Same Moon*, and *In the Shadow of the Moon* . . . not to mention the Harvest Moon Film Festival and the Full Moon Horror Film Festival!

PROPAGANDA MOVIES

The year 1950 saw America's first serious sci-fi Moon movies of the modern era. *Destination Moon* was a big-budget, full-color film about the United States' need to get to the Moon before the Soviets. A second film, *Rocketship X-M*, was a cheaper, more exciting black-and-white movie with a less aggressive message.

There is little plot in *Destination Moon*. The only real suspense is when the crew finds they don't have enough fuel to return from the Moon. The film's propaganda message is clear, though: America must colonize the Moon before the Communists make it a launchpad for missiles targeted at the US. In the movie world at least, the Space Race had started.

➔ Movie moonwalk in *Destination Moon*.

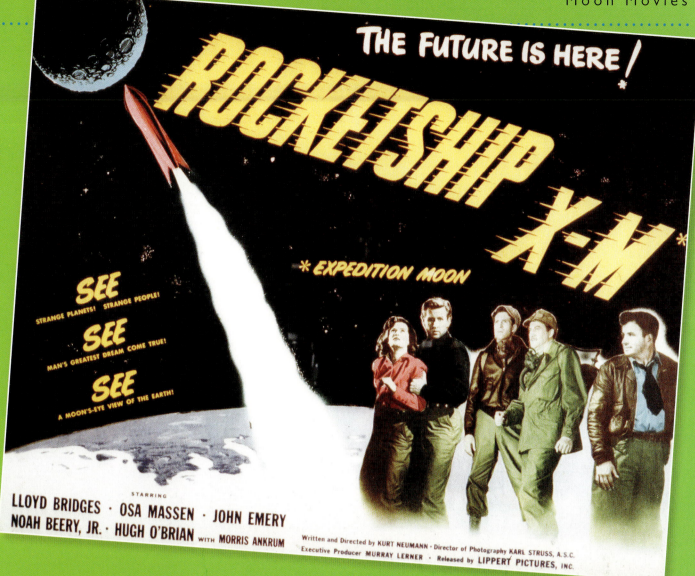

THE FUTURE IS HERE!

ROCKETSHIP X-M*

*EXPEDITION MOON

SEE
STRANGE PLANETS! STRANGE PEOPLE!

SEE
MAN'S GREATEST DREAM COME TRUE!

SEE
A MOON'S-EYE VIEW OF THE EARTH!

STARRING
LLOYD BRIDGES · OSA MASSEN · JOHN EMERY
NOAH BEERY, JR. · HUGH O'BRIAN with MORRIS ANKRUM

Written and Directed by KURT NEUMANN · Director of Photography KARL STRUSS, A.S.C.
Executive Producer MURRAY LERNER · Released by LIPPERT PICTURES, INC.

↑ Lobby card/poster for *Rocketship X-M*, 1950.

TERRIBLE WARNING

Destination Moon used nuclear power for its rocket ship, suggesting that nuclear was the fuel of the future. *Rocketship X-M* gave the opposite point of view. For complicated (and rather silly!) reasons, its mysteriously powered rocket shot past the Moon and ended up on Mars. Here the crew found evidence of a once-great civilization that had been destroyed in a nuclear war.

Made at the beginning of the Cold War between the US and the Soviet Union, and only five years after the nuclear destruction of the Japanese cities of Hiroshima and Nagasaki, *Rocketship X-M* issued a terrible warning: Nuclear power was not the answer to all humanity's problems; it might, in fact, destroy our entire civilization.

"That title is so good, you shouldn't even make the picture — you should just release the title!"

ACTOR AND DIRECTOR ORSON WELLES ON THE FILM TITLE *PAPER MOON*

MOON FLOPS

The 1974 Broadway musical *Man on the Moon* closed after just five nights. Nor was Moon exploration a successful comedy subject: the British film *Man in the Moon* (1961), starring Kenneth More, hardly got a laugh!

MOON HORROR

A full Moon hangs in a clear night sky. In its clean, cold light a lonely figure stumbles homeward across the desolate landscape. From far away comes the low howl of a wolf. The man stops, listening anxiously. A cloud slides silently over the face of the Moon, plunging the world into darkness. . . . The terrified traveler is doomed.

THE MOON CLICHÉ

Directors of horror films have made and remade this scene countless times. Vampire films, mummy films, zombie films . . . horror movies of every type — even a comic-horror *Simpsons* episode — make the Moon a symbol of evil. This has happened so often that the Moon as a sign of wickedness has become a film cliché.

Poor Moon! From *Death Moon* to *Full Moon Fright Night* and *Zombie Honeymoon*, the lifeless sphere of rock and dust is made responsible for every crime and beastliness imaginable. In *Black Moon* it allows a weird hag to have a squeaky conversation with a giant rat! And when a piece of stray meteor enters a man, as happens in *Track of the Moon Beast*, the innocent Moon is somehow at fault when the man turns into a monster!

⤴ *Fright Night*: The Moon hangs over a suburban nightmare in the 1985 horror movie.

NEW LEGENDS

The film industry used the Moon as an image of evil. Traditionally, our nearest neighbor was rarely associated with wickedness. Nasty things were sometimes said to happen when the Moon shone full, but normally people welcomed friendly moonlight.

Electric light started the change. When streets and homes were lit at the flick of a switch, moonlight was seen as unreliable and the Moon itself became associated with darkness instead of light.

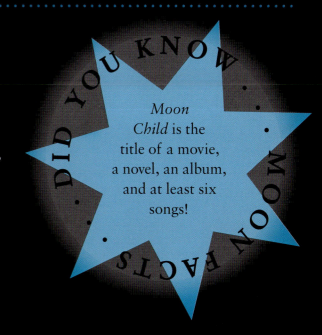

DID YOU KNOW · MOON FACTS

Moon Child is the title of a movie, a novel, an album, and at least six songs!

ONE IN THE EYE

The 1902 French film *A Trip to the Moon* is the earliest — and strangest — Moon movie. Mixing science fiction, fantasy, and classical mythology, it features a space rocket hitting the Man in the Moon in the eye!

⬆ Moon movie: *A Trip to the Moon* was the first film to cast the Moon in a starring role.

ON TARGET

Ten *Apollo* missions, manned and unmanned, paved the way for *Apollo 11*. Men, modules, rockets, and control systems were tested and analyzed in great detail. Things went wrong, of course, but happily nothing as serious as the *Apollo 1* disaster. Mistakes were sorted out and lessons learned so that by the summer of 1969, NASA was confident all was ready for the history-making voyage.

TRIUMPH OF SCIENCE

The first six *Apollo* missions were unmanned. They tested the rockets, including the titanic new *Saturn V*, and the thousands of pieces of other equipment required by the mission. Particularly significant was the development of computers, still comparatively new in the 1960s. They made the *Apollo* program possible because only a computer could quickly make all the calculations needed for vehicle testing and space flight.

It is difficult to imagine the precision required by the *Apollo* program. Engines more powerful than a thousand cars had to start and stop with split-second timing. While floating in space, the 33.1-ton (30-tonne) combined command and service modules had to re-dock with the 4.4-ton (4-tonne) lunar module — a maneuver of mind-boggling difficulty, like a person in a blindfold threading a needle while swimming in a rough sea.

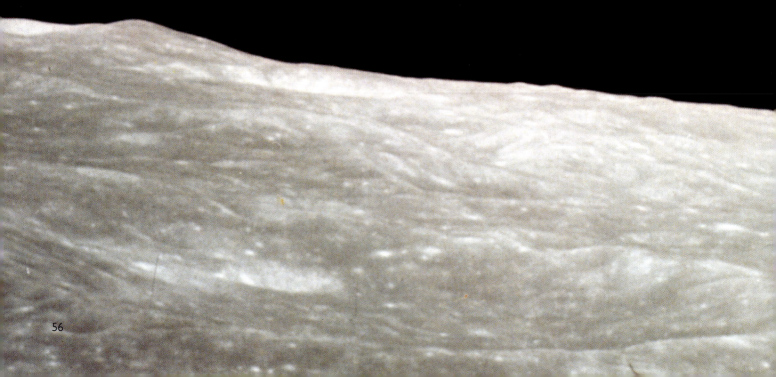

"*We came around the Moon for the very first time . . . and all of a sudden we saw the Earth come out of a lunar horizon. . . . I realized at that time just how insignificant we are in the Universe.*"

APOLLO 8 ASTRONAUT
JIM LOVELL,
ON SEEING EARTH RISE

TRIAL RUNS

Apollo 7 to *10* were manned voyages. *Apollo 7* placed a three-man command module in orbit around the Earth for nearly 11 days. *Apollo 8*, the first manned flight launched by *Saturn V*, saw three astronauts in lunar orbit. The broadcast they made from space in December 1968 was the most-watched TV program ever at the time. *Apollo 8* was the first time that humans saw the Earth rise above the horizon of another world.

Apollo 9 put a manned lunar module into Earth orbit. Finally, in May 1969, *Apollo 10* flew as a dummy run for the lunar landing itself. Once the three-man crew was in orbit around the Moon, the two-man lunar module flew down to within 9.5 miles (15.3 km) of its surface before returning to dock with the command module. The mission met with no major problems. The crew's safe return gave NASA the green light it had been waiting for – the Moon mission itself.

⬇ "The Spider": *Apollo 9*'s lunar module (LM), in which James McDivitt and Russell Schweickart orbited the Earth to test the vehicle's performance.

THE CHANGING MOON

Our view of the Moon changes night by night. These "phases" occur for two reasons. First, the Moon emits no light of its own: "Moonlight" is in fact the Sun's light reflected off the Moon. Second, the area lit up by the Sun varies as the Moon circles the Earth.

THE EIGHT PHASES OF THE MOON
Together these eight phases make up a full lunar month (about 29.5 days).

Waxing Gibbous Moon: almost there! So bright it can often be seen while the Sun is still shining.

First Quarter or Waxing Half-Moon: the Moon has completed a quarter of its journey around the Earth and 25 percent of it is visible until about midnight.

Waxing Crescent Moon: all we can see is a thin sliver of Moon — best viewed just after sunset.

New Moon: when the Moon is directly between the Earth and the Sun, so we can't see it at all.

SHAPES AND VIEWPOINTS

The Moon appears different when viewed from the Northern or Southern Hemisphere. A waxing crescent in the north, for instance, curves to the right. In the Southern Hemisphere the same Moon curves to the left.

Full Moon: the Sun lights up one half of the Moon, which shines with great brilliance all night.

Waning Gibbous Moon: on the wane, with the right side (Northern Hemisphere) sliding into darkness.

Last Quarter or Waning Half-Moon: the Moon, which has completed three-quarters of its journey around the Earth, rises after midnight and can still be seen in the morning.

Waning Crescent Moon: the final thin ribbon before the Moon disappears entirely from view (although it's still there, of course!) for three to four days.

AL-BIRUNI

Mega-bright Persian scholar al-Biruni (973–1048 CE) excelled at physics, geography, psychology, sociology, and medicine, as well as astronomy. Daringly, he accepted that the Moon's phases made sense if the Sun circled the Earth — or vice versa.

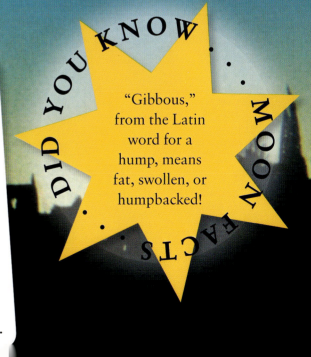

DID YOU KNOW... MOON FACTS

"Gibbous," from the Latin word for a hump, means fat, swollen, or humpbacked!

MOONLIT LOVE

The Moon's links with love and romance belong largely to Western culture. Other traditions — in Asia and Africa — respect the Moon but do not commonly associate it with love. This makes sense: The Moon's cold kingdom, the night, is rarely the right temperature for romance!

MOONLESS ROMANCE

After many years of hardship and pain, the Hindu god Rama was finally reunited with his wife, Sita. Overjoyed, they returned by night to their home city of Ayodhya. In the West, such a romantic homecoming would certainly have been made by moonlight. But that was not the Indian way.

Tradition says the night was so dark that Rama and Sita could not find their way. To help them, families marked the road by placing oil lamps outside their houses. So began Diwali, the Hindu Festival of Lights.

◒ Lighting the way: Lamps are lit to celebrate Diwali, the Hindu Festival of Lights.

MOONSTONE

This silvery blue stone, known to scientists as potassium aluminum silicate, is said to shine with captured moonbeams. In India it is sacred, representing the all-seeing Third Eye that brings wisdom and good fortune.

FLATTERING BEAMS

What is it about the Moon that makes Western poets, painters, and musicians go all sappy and weak-kneed? Maybe it is the quality of the light. By gentle moonlight, too soft to show blemishes and wrinkles, almost everyone can look charming. Or perhaps the Moon's links with romance are even more basic. After all, it appears at night, when secrets are hidden.

Whatever the reason, most love stories have a moonlit backdrop. When wandering Trojan hero Aeneas met Dido, Queen of Carthage . . . when Juliet fell in love with Romeo . . . when Danny and Sandy had "summer nights" in *Grease* . . . when romantic love was invented, moonlight was there to add its mysterious magic. And it has shone there ever since.

➋ Moonlight casts its spell over young lovers: Romeo and Juliet in a painting by John Bacon, 1905.

DID YOU KNOW . . . MOON FACTS

When someone is "mooning about," what's their problem? They're in love, of course!

ECLIPSE

Very occasionally, as the Earth and Moon spin around the Sun, all three line up. One of two things can then happen. Either the Moon prevents sunlight from reaching the Earth, or the Earth gets in the way of sunlight lighting up the Moon. Each event is known as an eclipse.

↑ Wounded moon: During a lunar eclipse, sunlight passing through Earth's atmosphere colors the Moon bloodred.

LUNAR ECLIPSE

A lunar eclipse is when the Earth passes between the Sun and the Moon. This happens at full Moon and makes for exciting viewing as Earth's huge shadow passes slowly across the Moon's silent face. We do not see a lunar eclipse every month because the Moon's path does not normally pass through the Earth's shadow.

The Earth's shadow is divided into two parts, the umbra and the penumbra. The umbra is the very darkest part of the shadow. A total lunar eclipse happens when the whole Moon passes through the umbra. The penumbra is the weaker part of the shadow. From here, only a partial eclipse is seen.

SOLAR ECLIPSE

A solar eclipse occurs when the Moon blots out the Sun. This can be very frightening as, for a few minutes, bright day is swiftly and mysteriously transformed to night. Like lunar eclipses, a solar eclipse may be total or partial.

There is another type of eclipse, called an annular eclipse. This occurs because the Moon's distance from Earth varies: When farthest away, it appears too small to cover the Sun completely. Instead, we see a bright ring (the annulus) of light gleaming around a darkened center.

In bygone ages, before people understood the science of eclipses, they were believed to herald some ghastly man-made or natural disaster. It is even reported that, in 585 BCE, an eclipse so scared two warring armies that they laid down their arms and made peace.

ECLIPSES ECLIPSED

The Moon is moving away from Earth at about 1.5 inches (3.8 cm) a year. In around 600 million years, therefore, it will be too distant to mask the Sun completely — so there will be no more total eclipses.

Light from the Sun travels toward Earth.

At any one time, an eclipse is visible from only a small area of Earth.

THE PIONEERS

By the time *Apollo 11* was ready to blast off on its historic mission, the United States had 26 men with spaceflight experience. Several had undertaken more than one mission. NASA had a good idea of the qualities needed in a successful astronaut and how best to train them for the greatest mission of all.

⬆ The chosen trio: from left, astronauts Neil Armstrong, Michael Collins, and Buzz Aldrin.

SELECTING THE BEST

There was certainly no shortage of candidates: Who wouldn't want to be the first man on the Moon? In the end, though, there could be just three. The men chosen were Edwin "Buzz" Aldrin, Neil Armstrong, and Michael Collins.

Over the years, NASA had selected three batches of men for astronaut training. Armstrong was in the second group, Aldrin and Collins in the third. Qualifications included superb physical fitness, total mental stability, a height of less than 5 feet 11 inches (1.8 m) tall (to fit into a small module), under the age of 40 (later reduced to 38), academically very well qualified, and, ideally, with experience flying fast jets.

The *Apollo 11* trio met all these requirements and more. Collins had been a test pilot. Aldrin was an ex–Korean War fighter pilot with a PhD in astronautics. Armstrong was also a Korean War pilot and had a master's degree in aerospace engineering. Together they were quite a team.

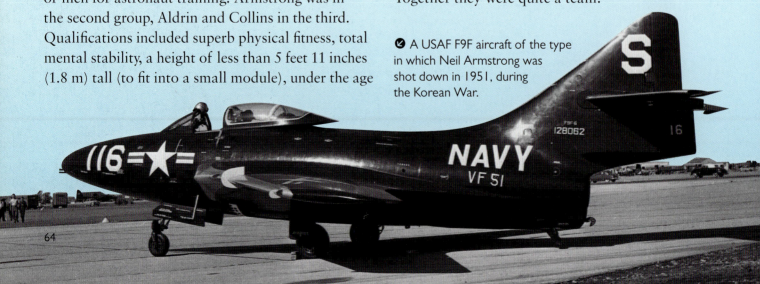

⬋ A USAF F9F aircraft of the type in which Neil Armstrong was shot down in 1951, during the Korean War.

TRAINING

Because they needed to report in detail on the Moon's surface, the astronauts were given a crash course in geology. They had 80 hours of classroom teaching and went on numerous field trips. At the same time, they received detailed instruction on the science of spaceflight and in their various craft.

Skills and physical training simulated every experience the astronauts might meet. They were made weightless in a diving plane, whirled around at high speed to get the feel of takeoff forces, and piloted mock-ups of the command and lunar modules. NASA even constructed an artificial "Moon surface" on which they could practice bringing down their lunar landing training vehicle (LLTV). When all this was finished, Aldrin, Armstrong, and Collins felt ready for anything.

➔ Moon practice: Wearing their space suits, Buzz Aldrin and Neil Armstrong train to use the tools they will take with them to the Moon.

DID YOU KNOW... MOON FACTS

Astronauts nicknamed the plane in which zero-gravity conditions were simulated the "Vomit Comet"!

A MATTER OF EXPERIENCE

All three of the *Apollo 11* astronauts had been on space missions before the Moon shot. Armstrong flew on *Gemini 8,* which performed the first docking in space. Collins had walked in space on *Gemini 10,* and Aldrin had piloted *Gemini 12* and spent 5.5 hours outside the vehicle. *Apollo 10* and *11* were the only missions on which all the crew members had previous space experience.

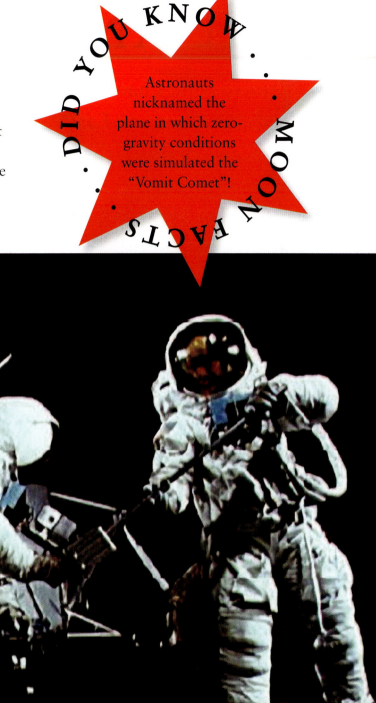

MOON MUSIC

He was a young man in love. Nothing very unusual in that, you may think. But his talent and ardor, combined with a secret illness and his girlfriend's social position, made sure that his passion — with a little help from a romantic-minded soldier-turned-writer — would endure forever.

MOONLIGHT SONATA

The fiery soul was the 31-year-old composer Ludwig van Beethoven. The object of his affection was one of his pupils, the talented 17-year-old Giulietta Guicciardi. The undisclosed illness was deeply tragic: Beethoven was slowly but certainly going deaf. Inspired by Giulietta's beauty and tormented by inner anxiety, he wrote a magnificent piano sonata and secretly dedicated it to her. Alas! Giulietta was a countess whose father refused to let her marry a poor composer, no matter how talented. Beethoven was heartbroken.

Writer Ludwig Rellstab is partly responsible for the lasting appeal and memory of Beethoven's ill-fated romance. Five years after the composer's death, he declared the sublime beginning of the Giulietta Guicciardi sonata to be a lover's vision of silvery moonlight gleaming on Switzerland's Lake Lucerne . . . and the name endures to this day: the *Moonlight Sonata*.

➋ Mister Moonlight: the outstanding romantic composer Ludwig van Beethoven (1770–1827).

TRAINING

Because they needed to report in detail on the Moon's surface, the astronauts were given a crash course in geology. They had 80 hours of classroom teaching and went on numerous field trips. At the same time, they received detailed instruction on the science of spaceflight and in their various craft.

Skills and physical training simulated every experience the astronauts might meet. They were made weightless in a diving plane, whirled around at high speed to get the feel of takeoff forces, and piloted mock-ups of the command and lunar modules. NASA even constructed an artificial "Moon surface" on which they could practice bringing down their lunar landing training vehicle (LLTV). When all this was finished, Aldrin, Armstrong, and Collins felt ready for anything.

➔ Moon practice: Wearing their space suits, Buzz Aldrin and Neil Armstrong train to use the tools they will take with them to the Moon.

DID YOU KNOW ... MOON FACTS

Astronauts nicknamed the plane in which zero-gravity conditions were simulated the "Vomit Comet"!

A MATTER OF EXPERIENCE

All three of the *Apollo 11* astronauts had been on space missions before the Moon shot. Armstrong flew on *Gemini 8*, which performed the first docking in space. Collins had walked in space on *Gemini 10*, and Aldrin had piloted *Gemini 12* and spent 5.5 hours outside the vehicle. *Apollo 10* and *11* were the only missions on which all the crew members had previous space experience.

TIME AND TIDE

Human beings have long realized that the Moon influences what happens on Earth. Its phases mark the passing of time and its beams brighten the darkest nights. Even more dramatic is its awesome power over the rising and falling of the oceans — the movements we know as tides.

MOON POWER

The reasons for the surging of the oceans around our coasts are extremely complicated. Basically, while land is fixed, the water on the surface of the Earth is free to move according to the forces acting on it. These include the spinning of the Earth and the pull of the Sun's gravity. Strongest of all, however, is the Moon's gravity.

Although the Moon is far smaller than the Sun, its gravity has twice the effect on the sea because it is so much nearer to the Earth (about 238,855 miles [384,400 km] as opposed to 92,584,300 miles [149,000,000 km]). This means that the seas nearest to the Moon are pulled slightly toward it. At the same time, the seas on the other side of the Earth bulge away.

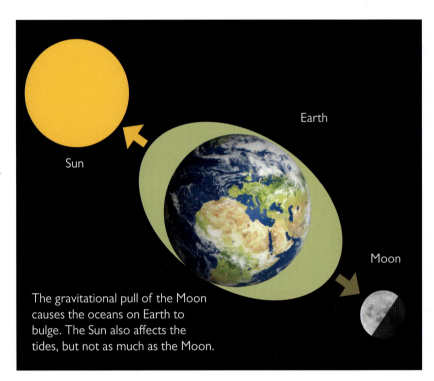

The gravitational pull of the Moon causes the oceans on Earth to bulge. The Sun also affects the tides, but not as much as the Moon.

SPRING AND NEAP TIDES

Tides do not rise and fall by regular amounts. The weather, currents, and the shape of the coastline all play their parts. The biggest variation between high and low water is called a spring tide. This has nothing to do with the season but happens at full and new Moons, and when the Sun, Earth, and Moon are aligned.

A neap tide is when the difference between high and low water is at its smallest. This occurs during quarter Moons (see page 58). The biggest spring tides happen at the equinoxes — twice a year, when the lengths of day and night are equal.

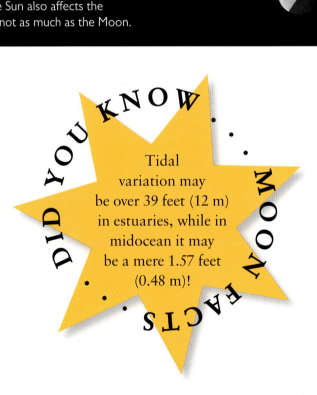

DID YOU KNOW MOON FACTS

Tidal variation may be over 39 feet (12 m) in estuaries, while in midocean it may be a mere 1.57 feet (0.48 m)!

⬆ Moon power: Low (above) and high (below) tides are obvious signs of the Moon's influence on our world.

MOON MUSIC

He was a young man in love. Nothing very unusual in that, you may think. But his talent and ardor, combined with a secret illness and his girlfriend's social position, made sure that his passion — with a little help from a romantic-minded soldier-turned-writer — would endure forever.

MOONLIGHT SONATA

The fiery soul was the 31-year-old composer Ludwig van Beethoven. The object of his affection was one of his pupils, the talented 17-year-old Giulietta Guicciardi. The undisclosed illness was deeply tragic: Beethoven was slowly but certainly going deaf. Inspired by Giulietta's beauty and tormented by inner anxiety, he wrote a magnificent piano sonata and secretly dedicated it to her. Alas! Giulietta was a countess whose father refused to let her marry a poor composer, no matter how talented. Beethoven was heartbroken.

Writer Ludwig Rellstab is partly responsible for the lasting appeal and memory of Beethoven's ill-fated romance. Five years after the composer's death, he declared the sublime beginning of the Giulietta Guicciardi sonata to be a lover's vision of silvery moonlight gleaming on Switzerland's Lake Lucerne . . . and the name endures to this day: the *Moonlight Sonata*.

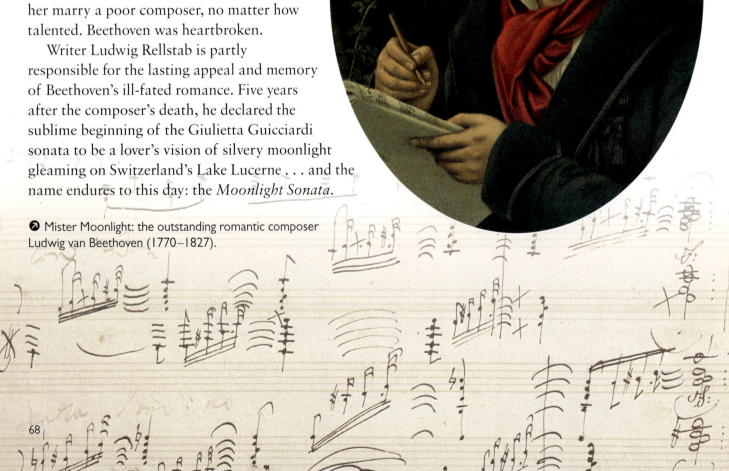

⟳ Mister Moonlight: the outstanding romantic composer Ludwig van Beethoven (1770–1827).

CLAIR DE LUNE

Other composers, such as Americans Edward MacDowell and Dennis Ruff, and Frenchman Claude Debussy, have written Moon-inspired works. Debussy's lovely piano piece *Clair de Lune* ("Moonlight," 1903) has become almost as popular as Beethoven's sonata. The tune has been featured in over a dozen films, ranging from *Pinocchio* to *Atonement*, and has also been heard in episodes of *The Simpsons*, on rock albums, and in Game Boy games! Whatever the medium, the magic of the Moon has clearly lost none of its mysterious power.

DID YOU KNOW . . . MOON FACTS

Opera della Luna ("Opera of the Moon") is a successful modern opera company — on Earth!

➲ *Atonement* was one of many films to use Debussy's *Clair de Lune*.

ZERO HOUR

By breakfast on July 16, 1969, a crowd of one million people crowded the highways, beaches, and open spaces surrounding the Kennedy Space Center. Around the world another 500 million watched on TV as the clock ticked slowly toward zero hour. At precisely 09:32 local time, five engines thundering and their flames scorching the surrounding marshland, the mighty *Saturn* V rose majestically into the warm Florida air. Awestruck, the onlookers broke into relieved applause.

Destination Moon! With the eyes of the world upon it, *Apollo 11* lifts off the launchpad at the start of its historic journey.

DID YOU KNOW ... MOON FACTS

The *Saturn V*'s power was so frightening that at takeoff Armstrong's heartbeat rose to 109 per minute!

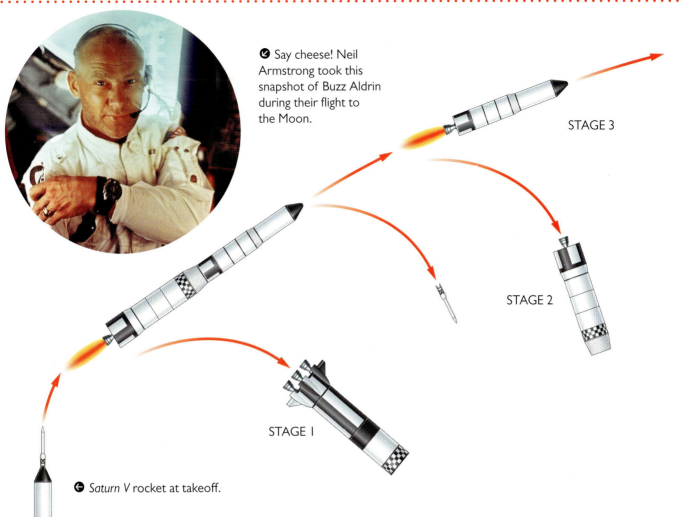

Say cheese! Neil Armstrong took this snapshot of Buzz Aldrin during their flight to the Moon.

STAGE 3

STAGE 2

STAGE 1

Saturn V rocket at takeoff.

STAGE 1

High above the fire and noise, the three astronauts strapped into the command module were pushed farther back into their chairs as the vast machine gathered speed. After just 2.5 minutes, already traveling faster than any conventional plane, the central engine stopped. Fifteen seconds later, the four outer engines also cut out and, precisely one second after that, the stage housing them separated from the speeding rocket above. Eight small motors fired briefly to push the discarded first stage back toward the Earth, already 38 miles (61 km) below.

STAGE 2

The second stage hurled *Apollo 11* toward the speed of 17,398 mph (28,000 km/h) required to stay in Earth orbit. It too had five engines,

and these burned for six minutes before they stopped and their stage fell away. The craft was now 115 miles (185 km) above the Earth. A burn of precisely 2 minutes 45 seconds from the third stage's single engine was all that was needed to put *Apollo* into orbit.

STAGE 3

So far the mission had been controlled either automatically or from the ground. The crew's task was to stay cool and check that all was running smoothly. After one-and-a-half orbits of Earth, *Apollo* had been airborne for 2 hours and 45 minutes, and it was time to accelerate once more. The third stage fired again, this time for 5 minutes and 47 seconds. *Apollo* sped to 224,544 mph (361,369 km/h), freeing it from Earth's gravity and sending it down the long path toward the distant Moon.

71

MOON SONG

What is it about the Moon that makes people of all cultures want to burst into song? The Jews had a traditional lyric about the Moon, the Irish about the "Rising of the Moon," and the Hungarians about a "Very Big Moon." As for modern Moon songs . . . the list is endless.

MOONRAKER

The 1979 James Bond film *Moonraker* bred a song of the same name. It is not widely known, however, that in Kent, England, "Moonrakers" were once smugglers — men who raked ponds by moonlight to retrieve hidden loot.

BLUE MOON

The most popular Moon song is the 1934 hit "Blue Moon." Its Moon link was a bit slow to appear: The composer, Richard Rodgers, came up with the tune in the summer of 1933, but another year passed before lyricist Lorenz Hart finally wrote the famous words.

"Blue moon / You saw me standing alone . . ." was Hart's fourth attempt to find lyrics that suited the melody. After that, the song became a worldwide favorite. It has featured in numerous films, has topped the music charts, and has been translated into dozens of languages. Elvis Presley made it a rock song, the movie *An American Werewolf in London* used three different versions of it, and the Manchester City Football Club adopted it as their official song.

🌙 Howling at the Moon: *An American Werewolf in London* used the song "Blue Moon" as a recurring theme.

MOONSPIRATION

As the charts show, you can't keep the Moon down!

1930s
Connecticut Collegians: "Drifting Under a Summer Moon" (1932)
Glen Miller: "Moonlight Serenade" (1939)

1940s
Frank Sinatra: "The Moon Was Yellow" (1945)
Bill Monroe: "Blue Moon of Kentucky" (1947)

1950s
Ella Fitzgerald: "It's Only a Paper Moon" (1955)
Gale Storm: "Dark Moon" (1957)

1960s
Beach Boys: "Surfer Moon" (1963)
Grateful Dead: "Mountains of the Moon" (1969)

1970s
Paul McCartney: "'C' Moon" (1972)
Police: "Walking on the Moon" (1979)

1980s
Paul Simon: "Song About the Moon" (1981)
Sting: "Sister Moon" (1987)

1990s
R.E.M.: "Man on the Moon" (1992)
Emerson, Lake & Palmer: "Black Moon" (1992)

2000s
LeAnn Rimes: "Can't Fight the Moonlight" (2000)
Kaiser Chiefs: "Moon" (2003)

⊙ The band Kaiser Chiefs, whose song "Moon" followed in a long tradition of lunar tunes.

DID YOU KNOW ... MOON FACTS

American legend Frank Sinatra recorded more Moon songs than any other vocal artist.

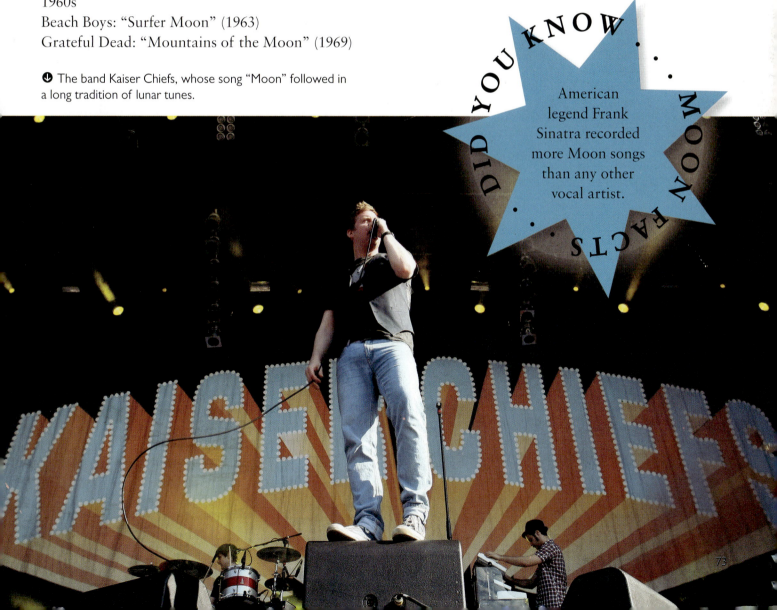

MOON MATTER

The Moon is like an enormous bull's-eye with three layers. Around the outside lies a light crust between 37 and 62 miles (60 and 100 km) thick. Beneath this, making up the bulk of the Moon, is a heavier mantle. At the very center there appears to be a metallic core, about 497 miles (800 km) across.

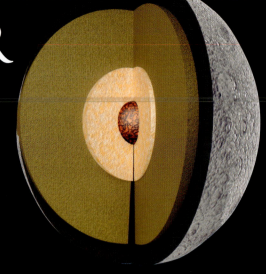

⬆ Like a huge apple, the Moon has a skin (the crust), an inner bulk (the mantle), and a core.

LOW GRUMBLINGS

It seems certain that the Moon was once molten — a spinning ball of liquid, gas, and rock. While it was in that state, the heavier matter sank toward the core, leaving the lighter material nearer the surface. It was this that the *Apollo 11* astronauts gathered as samples.

Although it may still have molten matter at its core, most of the Moon cooled down and solidified ages ago. Unlike the Earth, it has no moving plates of crust and, probably, no active volcanoes. Surprisingly, though, there are still moonquakes: low grumblings and grindings that rumble away 621 miles (1,000 km) below the lifeless surface. They are most likely caused by temperature changes, shifts in Earth–Moon gravity, and the impact of large asteroids.

⬅ Fishing for chips: On the rim of Plumb Crater, *Apollo 16* astronaut John W. Young chips samples from a lunar boulder for analysis back on Earth.

MOON MINERAL

The *Apollo 11* astronauts found one Moon mineral that did not exist on Earth. It was given the name "armacolite," made up of the first letters of their surnames: Armstrong, Aldrin, and Collins.

MOON GARDENING

The Earth's atmosphere wraps around it like a blanket, sustaining life and shielding it from damaging bombardment. The Moon's thin atmosphere affords no such defense. This leaves it open to a rain of alien matter arriving from elsewhere in the galaxy.

Particles ranging in size from single electrons to huge asteroids are continually splattering down onto the Moon. The larger impacts carve out enormous craters, while the smaller ones just dig up the surface. Scientists describe this process as lunar "gardening," giving the Moon a glassy gray "soil," (called a regolith) that looks and feels rather like cement powder.

DID YOU KNOW... MOON FACTS

The tiny amounts of water found on the Moon may have arrived in bodies crashing in from outer space.

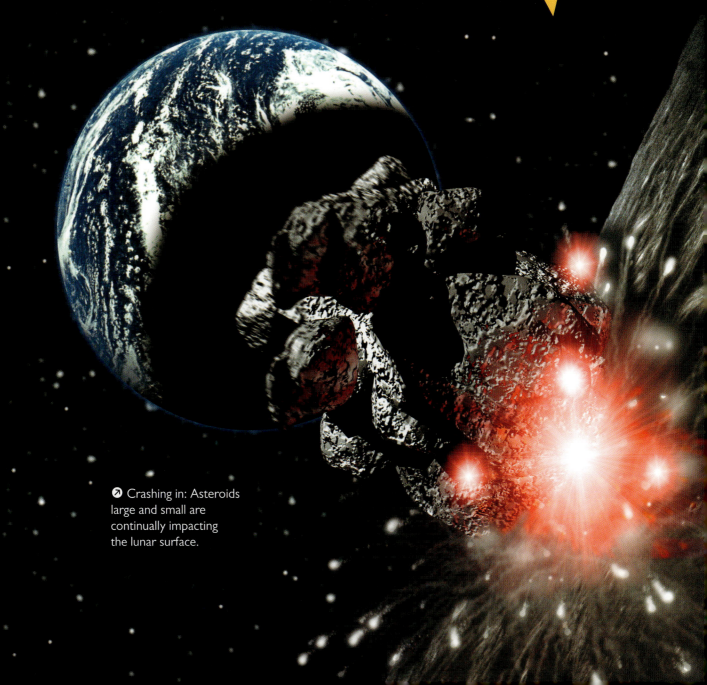

⬈ Crashing in: Asteroids large and small are continually impacting the lunar surface.

HERE WE COME!

Apollo 11 was now down to four units. The lunar module (LM) sat above the third stage of the *Saturn* rocket. Next came the service module (SM), providing the electricity and air, and storing the crew's food and water. At the front was the manned command module (CM).

ABOUT-FACE

With *Apollo 11* on course for the Moon, the crew detach their joint command and service module (CSM) and let it drift away a short distance.

They then turn it around 180 degrees so that its nose points toward the hatch in the LM.

The CSM edges up to the LM until the two can be firmly joined together, hatch to hatch, with an airtight seal. The discarded stage-three rocket now drifts off.

This leaves the CSM with the LM on its nose, the whole thing looking like a spider sitting on top of a stubby pen. Finally, after the craft has swung around so the SM's engine is at the back, *Apollo 11* continues on its historic journey.

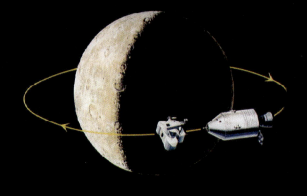

MODULE LIVING

The CM in which the crew lived was shaped like a topless cone, 10.5 feet (3.2 m) tall and 12.8 feet (3.9 m) in diameter across the bottom. Packed with levers, dials, switches, and lights, it was hardly a comfort zone. In this tiny space three grown men had to work, eat, relieve themselves, and sleep (one at a time). They were weightless, too, so they and everything else floated about unless fixed down. Eating mostly dull-tasting dehydrated meals and vitamin pills, the astronauts lost interest in food and returned lighter than when they had set out. Small wonder some astronauts became grumpy!

➲ All aboard! The crew of *Apollo 11* checking equipment and storage space within their command module.

NEIL ARMSTRONG

Flying was in Neil Armstrong's (b. 1930) blood. He got a pilot's license on his sixteenth birthday, qualified in aerospace engineering, and flew for the US Navy before captaining *Apollo 11*. After leaving NASA, he became a college lecturer.

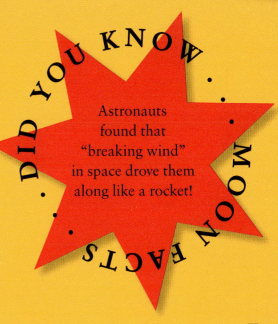

DID YOU KNOW... MOON FACTS

Astronauts found that "breaking wind" in space drove them along like a rocket!

THE *EAGLE* HAS LANDED!

Apollo 11 reached the Moon in three days. At first, the Earth's gravity pulled it back, slowing it to just 1,988 mph (3,200 km/h). But when lunar gravity came into play, it sped up again. Had the crew not used the SM engine as a brake, they would have shot off into distant space!

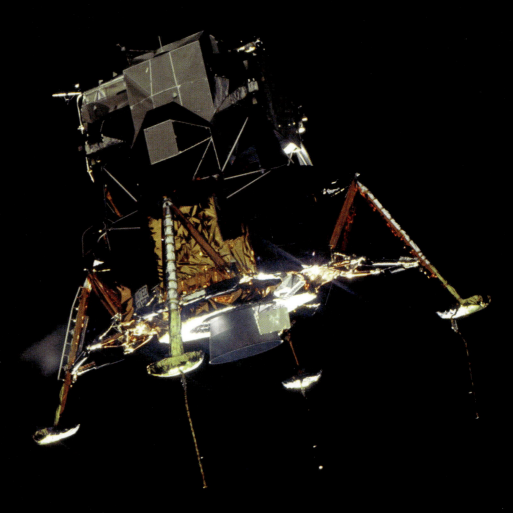

Eagle, the lunar module, ready for its Moon landing. Note its two-part structure and the probes below its legs.

INTO THE *EAGLE*

With *Apollo 11* in low lunar orbit, the crew checked their landing place in the Sea of Tranquility. NASA had chosen this site because it appeared flat and smooth. When all was ready, Armstrong and Aldrin said good-bye to Collins and climbed into the lunar module. Hatches sealed and last checks made, the lunar module — *Eagle* — then eased away from the CSM — *Columbia* — in which Collins was now alone. After a few somersaults in front of Collins so he could check for damage, the *Eagle* began its descent.

THE DESCENT

The *Eagle* was in two sections. The larger, four-legged descent module (22,783 pounds [10,334 kg]), situated at the bottom, could land on the Moon under its own power. The smaller ascent module (10,869 pounds [4,930 kg]), which rode piggyback on the descent module, was to carry the astronauts back to *Columbia*.

Piloted by Buzz Aldrin, the *Eagle* slowly edged toward the chosen landing ground. With only about 328 feet (100 m) to go, he suddenly realized that what had looked smooth from a distance was actually covered with large boulders. Unfazed, he searched around and found a safer spot. Just above the surface he cut the engine and, 102 hours 45 minutes and 40 seconds after takeoff, *Apollo 11* was on the Moon. "Houston, Tranquility Base here," radioed Armstrong to the command center in Texas. "The *Eagle* has landed."

"I'd like to take this opportunity to ask every person listening in . . . to pause for a moment and contemplate the events of the past few hours and give thanks in his or her own way."

BUZZ ALDRIN, AFTER LANDING ON THE MOON

→ We've made it! The lunar module on the surface of the Moon.

← The folks back home: Every stage of the *Apollo 11* mission was monitored and controlled by the Kennedy Space Center, Florida, and Mission Control, Houston, Texas.

MOON MAP

While around 70 percent of the Earth's surface is water-covered, the Moon is all land. It does not have — and probably never did have — oceans, rivers, or lakes. Like the Earth, though, it does have mountains, valleys, and plains. Early astronomers called the latter seas, or "*maria*," because that is what they looked like from Earth.

SURFACE SMALLPOX

The surface of the Moon looks like the skin of someone who has suffered from the disease smallpox. Space bombardment has produced craters of all sizes. The flat-bottomed inside of a large crater is called a basin or "mare." The biggest and newest, known as South Pole–Aitken, is around 1,553 miles (2,500 km) across and 8 miles (13 km) deep. The object that produced it must have been gigantic — as big as a country.

Most of the Moon's hills and mountain ranges were formed from the debris thrown up by an impact, not from ancient volcanoes. Lunar lava was much thinner than Earth lava, so it flowed away quickly instead of piling up into new mountains.

⬆ In this special colored picture of the Moon, the blue areas are plains (maria), the reds are highlands, and the yellowish area at the bottom is the gigantic South Pole–Aitken crater.

⬇ Lunar lava: an artist's impression of how the Moon may have looked when it was volcanically active.

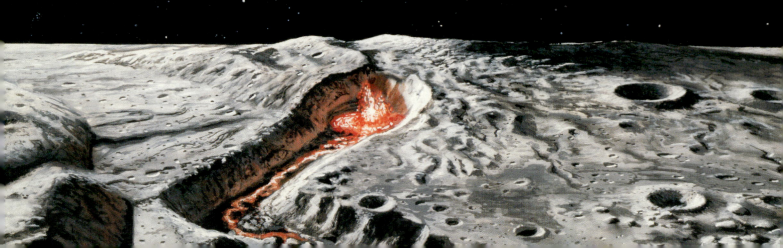

MOON MYSTERIES

Several features of the moonscape have yet to be explained. Why, for example, are the mountains on the dark side an average of 1.1 miles (1.8 km) higher than those on the side facing Earth? What are those strange swirly patterns, such as Reiner Gamma, that appear on the lunar surface? No one knows.

The most perplexing lunar feature is the rille. Rilles, which can be twisty or straight, are dry valleys running across the surface. The largest, named Schröter's Valley, meanders for hundreds of miles then stops abruptly. Was it a river of lava? And if it was, then where did all that flowing lava go?

⬆ Moon mystery: Unexplained swirly patterns — Reiner Gamma — on the lunar surface.

⬅ The strange lunar rille known as Schröter's Valley. Scientists are unsure how it was formed.

DID YOU KNOW . . . MOON FACTS

Objects strike the Moon with such tremendous force that they and the lunar surface melt on impact.

THE WHITE BEAUTY

Throughout history, the Moon has inspired poets of every land and of every tongue to write of love and longing. Here, mostly in translation, are some moving examples of how our souls have been stirred.

GERMAN

Not stars, not sun, not
moonbeams sweet,
Could make my heart
with rapture beat.
'Tis love alone that
smilingly
Peers forth from Nature's
blissful eye,
As from a mirror ever!

Friedrich Schiller, from
"The Triumph of Love"

AMERICAN

The moon was but a chin of gold
A night or two ago,
And now she turns her perfect face
Upon the world below.
Her forehead is of amplest blond;
Her cheek like beryl stone;
Her eye unto the summer dew
The likest I have known.

Emily Dickinson, from "The Moon"

FRENCH

Upon a darkening night,
Above the yellow tower sat
The Moon,
Like a dot upon an i.

Are you the eye of blinkered sky?
What cunning cherubim
Spies on us
From behind your pallid mask?

Alfred de Musset, from "Ballad
to the Moon"

ENGLISH

Art thou pale for weariness
Of climbing heaven and gazing on the Earth,
Wandering companionless
Among the stars that have a different birth,
And ever changing, like a joyless eye
That finds no object worth its constancy?

Percy Bysshe Shelley, from "To the Moon"

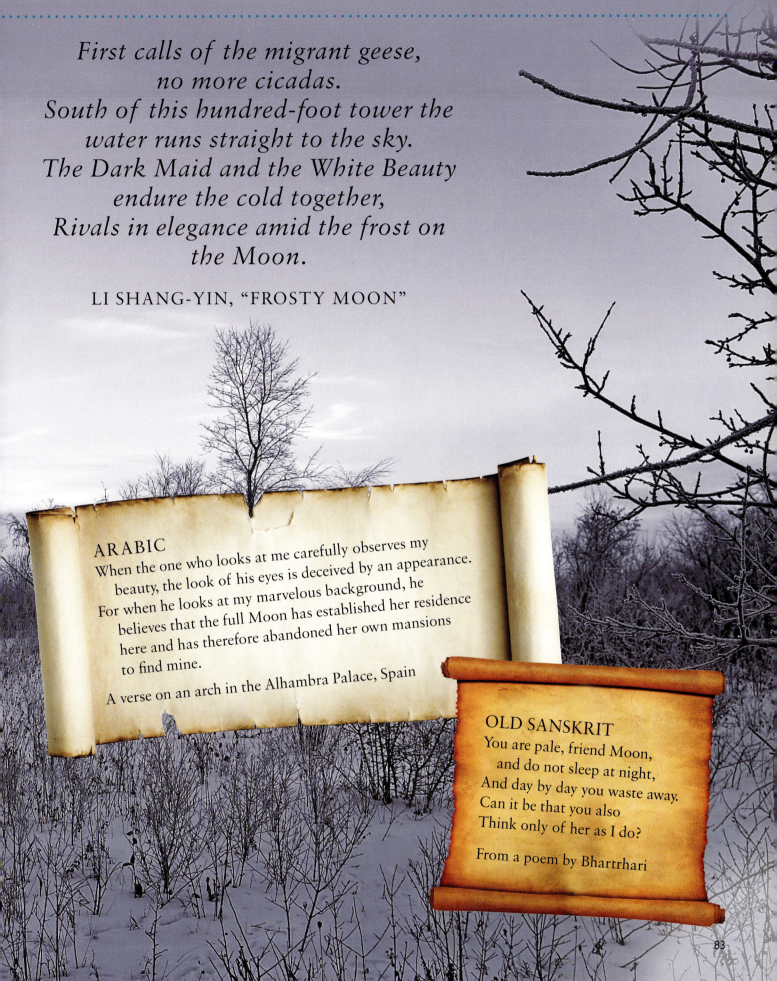

First calls of the migrant geese,
no more cicadas.
South of this hundred-foot tower the
water runs straight to the sky.
The Dark Maid and the White Beauty
endure the cold together,
Rivals in elegance amid the frost on
the Moon.

LI SHANG-YIN, "FROSTY MOON"

ARABIC

When the one who looks at me carefully observes my beauty, the look of his eyes is deceived by an appearance. For when he looks at my marvelous background, he believes that the full Moon has established her residence here and has therefore abandoned her own mansions to find mine.

A verse on an arch in the Alhambra Palace, Spain

OLD SANSKRIT

You are pale, friend Moon,
   and do not sleep at night,
And day by day you waste away.
Can it be that you also
Think only of her as I do?

From a poem by Bhartrhari

ONE SMALL STEP

It took Armstrong and Aldrin over six hours to leave the module. One reason for this was a problem with the exit hatch. The designers had reduced its diameter but left the astronaut's equipment the same size. The two men almost found themselves on the Moon but unable to get out and look around!

⬆ It's so easy on Earth: Neil Armstrong practices climbing down the lunar module ladder.

INTO THE *EAGLE*

Trying not to think about what lay outside, the astronauts went through a detailed check of their module and equipment. Both men were now wearing their space suits, with bulky Portable Life Support Systems (PLSSs) on their backs and Remote Control Units (RCUs) on their chests. When all was ready, they switched their air hoses from the module's supply to those in the PLSS backpacks. Then, slowly and carefully, they opened the hatch and peered out at the grim desert on all sides. It was very still . . . utterly lifeless.

Armstrong went first, eventually squeezing backward through the hatch. Because his RCU stuck out so far, he could not see where he was putting his feet on the ladder. After all that training, rehearsal, and expenditure, it is extraordinary that such basic errors had still been made!

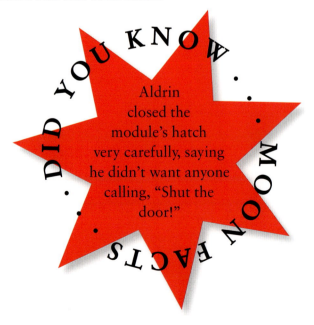

DID YOU KNOW . . . MOON FACTS

Aldrin closed the module's hatch very carefully, saying he didn't want anyone calling, "Shut the door!"

DOWN THE LADDER

Before he climbed down, Armstrong switched on a TV camera attached to one of the module's legs. Sound and blurry images were relayed back to Earth, where an estimated 650 million people watched in amazement and wonder as a man prepared to stand on the Moon. The surface below him, Armstrong reported, looked like powdered charcoal. He was now at the foot of the ladder. From here he lowered his left foot to the dusty surface, leaving a deep imprint, and uttered his famous words.

"That's one small step for man, one giant leap for mankind."

NEIL ARMSTRONG
AS HE STEPPED
ONTO THE MOON

➔ Armstrong carefully negotiates the module's ladder.

DRAMATIC MOON

There are almost as many plays about the Moon as there are songs and films on the subject. Like other creative artists, playwrights use the Moon as a symbol. They borrow from each other, too: *The Moon Is Down*, the title of John Steinbeck's successful play, novel, and film, comes from Shakespeare's play *Macbeth*.

RING AROUND THE MOON

The best-known modern Moon play is *Ring Around the Moon*, a criticism of old-world snobbery by the French playwright Jean Anouilh. Actually, its correct title is *L'Invitation au Château* ("The Invitation to the Country House," 1947). It gained its Moon link only when adapted by the English writer Christopher Fry in 1950.

Another modern Moon play is Harold Pinter's *Moonlight* (1993). It concerns a dying man and his relationship with his wife and sons. There is no romance in this moonlight, just the cold and bleak loneliness of age and the steady approach of death.

➲ *Fanstasy World Under the Moon*: a poster by Jules Cheret for the Musée Grévin (wax museum) in Paris.

MOON DREAMERS

Who lived in "Starry Up"? The Moon Dreamers, fantasy characters in a 1980s TV drama. Their job? To see that all the children living on the distant planet Earth had sweet dreams every night.

⬆ Moonlit midsummer madness: In Shakespeare's *A Midsummer Night's Dream*, Titania, Queen of the Fairies, falls in love with Bottom, a donkey-eared country bumpkin.

"This lantern doth the horned moon present;
Myself the Man i' th' Moon do seem to be."

THE TAILOR STARVELING IN SHAKESPEARE'S
A MIDSUMMER NIGHT'S DREAM

LUNAR ATMOSPHERE

Compared with Earth, the Moon doesn't really have an atmosphere. Scientifically speaking, though, it does have one — but only just. It is unbelievably thin and certainly lacks the life-sustaining mix of gases that we enjoy. Moreover, the lunar atmosphere presents us with a number of puzzles.

DULL STUFF

The Moon's feeble atmosphere is billions of times lighter than Earth's. It is mostly made up of tiny quantities of dull gases like neon, helium, and argon. These elements go by the flattering name of "noble." In fact, they do very little: They are colorless, odorless, and inactive.

More interesting are the small quantities of radon found in the Moon's atmosphere. As its name suggests, this gas is released when radioactive bits of the Moon decay. There are also tiny traces of other gases floating around above the Moon's surface. Hydrogen has been identified, for example. There are even small amounts of gases that feature prominently in our atmosphere: oxygen and carbon dioxide. How they got there, no one knows.

◐ Lunar scooper: *Apollo 17* astronaut Harrison Schmitt, a geologist, uses a special tool to collect samples of Moon soil.

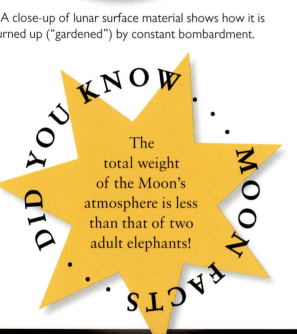

⬆ A close-up of lunar surface material shows how it is churned up ("gardened") by constant bombardment.

JUST A SPLASH

With the Moon under constant bombardment (see pages 74–75), tiny bits of its surface — often no larger than an atom or two — are always splashing upward. This may be how aluminum and silicon molecules enter the lunar atmosphere. They are most likely to be splashed up when the bright side of the Moon is enjoying one of its two-week-long periods of sunlight. There is dust floating around above the surface, too. With no wind to keep the dust aloft, scientists believe static electricity prevents it from falling back to the bleakness below.

DID YOU KNOW . . . MOON FACTS

The total weight of the Moon's atmosphere is less than that of two adult elephants!

LUNAR POLLUTION

The *Apollo 11* astronauts left instruments on the Moon's surface to measure its atmosphere. Unfortunately, they picked up the pollution caused by the lunar module's engines, making their evidence rather unreliable.

Buzz Aldrin lifts scientific equipment that would have been too heavy to carry on Earth.

❯ The beauty of space: moonrise over the blue haze of Earth's atmosphere.

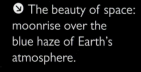

MEN FROM EARTH

As the Moon landing was a scientific mission, Armstrong quickly set about picking up pieces of rock and soil. This was in case something went wrong and he had to cut short his stay. All was well, however, and soon Aldrin joined him for two and a half hours of data collection.

TREASURE HUNT

The two pioneers photographed, tested for surface wind, took temperature readings, drilled into the ground, and gathered 47.8 pounds (21.7 kg) of mineral samples. Back on Earth, doctors monitored the men carefully, noting how their bodies were coping with the extraordinary environment. At one point they told Armstrong to slow down: All the rushing around had sent his metabolic rate rather high.

As planned, the astronauts left souvenirs from Earth. The most striking was an American flag, which had a wire support along the top to make it look as if it were blowing in the wind.

LOPING

The human body has adapted to life on Earth, so scientists were unsure how it would cope with gravity only one-sixth the strength of that on our planet. For example, the astronauts had to find the best way of getting around. They tried several ways, including kangaroo-style leaps, before opting for hopping along with huge strides. This was not easy, though, because their heavy packs tended to tip them over backward. Also, being so light and moving so fast, it was difficult to stop quickly. To avoid crashes, they planned their moves five or six steps ahead — taking great care not to trip over the TV cable they had set up.

⬆ Aldrin beside the American flag that was designed to "fly" in a windless atmosphere.

⬅ Loping along on the low-gravity Moon took a bit of getting used to.

EDWIN "BUZZ" ALDRIN

Moving from the US Air Force to NASA, pilot Buzz Aldrin (b. 1930) soon adapted to the controls of the lunar module. Later, he wrote and lectured about the Moon landing experience — and Buzz Lightyear was named after him in the movie Toy Story.

LUNAR GRAVITY

On the Moon we all weigh about six times less than on Earth. It's a great place for records, too. A 1-foot (0.3 m) earthly jump becomes 6 feet (1.8 m) high on the Moon. These differences occur because the Moon's gravity is six times weaker than Earth's.

DID YOU KNOW · **MOON FACTS**

A person's weight is less on the Moon, although their mass is the same.

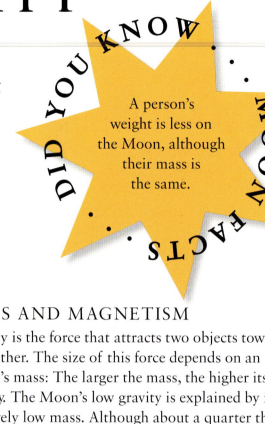

Early learning: A 1963 *Life* magazine features US astronauts training to eat in weightless conditions.

MASS AND MAGNETISM

Gravity is the force that attracts two objects toward each other. The size of this force depends on an object's mass: The larger the mass, the higher its gravity. The Moon's low gravity is explained by its relatively low mass. Although about a quarter the Earth's size, it has only one-sixth of its gravity.

The Moon is also lopsided. The center of its mass is not in the middle, and some crust regions have greater mass than others. Lunar gravity, therefore, varies from place to place. Magnetism is another Earth-Moon difference. While the Earth's iron-rich core makes our planet a gigantic magnet, the Moon has no iron core and no magnetic field.

WEIGHT LOSS

The Moon's low gravity is still strong enough to affect the movement of the Earth. As a result, the Moon does not simply orbit the Earth — the two bodies actually orbit each other. At the same time, they are both going around the Sun.

The Earth and Moon orbit the Sun as if they were one body, with one mass. The center of this Earth-Moon mass (known as the "barycenter") lies about 2,920 miles (4,700 km) from the center of the Earth. Astronomers plotting the Earth's orbit around the Sun need to base their calculations not on the center of the Earth but on the barycenter.

Learning to walk again: The *Apollo 11* astronauts had to find a new way of getting around on the low-gravity Moon.

LUNACY

Since ancient times, superstitions and stories have linked crazy human behavior to the full Moon. The English word "lunatic," meaning "mad person," actually comes from *luna*, Latin for the Moon. Although scientists say such ideas are nonsense, millions honestly believe that the Moon influences the way we behave.

◀ Lunatic London: a sinister scene beside the River Thames (1910).

POSSIBLE EXPLANATION

There are still experts who claim that more thefts, murders, arson, road accidents, suicides, and other unpleasant things happen at the full Moon than at other times. As evidence, they put forward statistical studies. Their opponents offer statistics that show no link between antisocial behavior and the Moon.

There is a theory that might explain the mystery. When the Moon is full and bright, people tend to sleep less well. This is because our senses are confused between night and day. And when we sleep badly, we get grouchy — and perhaps do things we would not usually do. All because of the Moon.

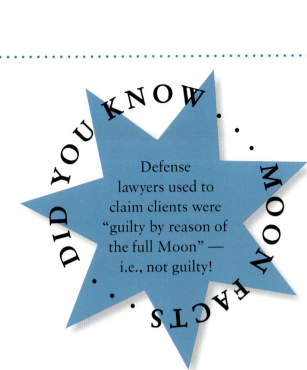

Defense lawyers used to claim clients were "guilty by reason of the full Moon" — i.e., not guilty!

*Demoniac frenzy,
moping melancholy
And moon-struck madness.*

POET JOHN MILTON

BRAIN TIDES

Those who claim that human conduct is affected by the phases of the Moon normally base their theories on two facts. Firstly, our bodies are about 60 percent water. Secondly, the Moon's gravity is powerful enough to influence great quantities of water in the oceans, producing tides. So, the argument runs, just as the full Moon helps produce the highest tides, it must also affect the water in our bodies, especially in our brains. These "brain tides" make us act out of character . . . turning us into lunatics!

Actually, the gravity of a brick wall 1 foot (0.3 m) away has more power over our body's water than the Moon.

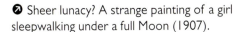 Sheer lunacy? A strange painting of a girl sleepwalking under a full Moon (1907).

HOMEWARD BOUND

As things had gone so well, Armstrong and Aldrin were given an extra 15 minutes on the Moon's surface. At the end of this period, they climbed carefully back up the ladder into the ascent stage, hauling their boxes of film and rock samples with them on a pulley system.

MOMENT OF TRUTH

The tiny cabin of the lunar module's ascent stage was packed with instruments. Struggling around inside in his bulky space suit, Buzz Aldrin accidentally hit the switch that prepared the engine for takeoff. For a few dreadful seconds, the astronauts and ground control feared the engine could not be restarted: The astronauts would slowly suffocate in their module tomb. Happily, the problem was solved after a bit of nifty work with a felt pen! Relieved, the two men threw out unwanted heavy equipment, sealed the module, repressurized it, and lay down for a well-deserved rest.

Neil Armstrong working with the lunar module's bewildering array of controls and displays.

REUNITED

Mission Control in Houston, Texas, woke the astronauts seven hours later. It took a couple of hours to prepare for takeoff, at the end of which the ascent stage's rocket engine started without a hitch. Using the descent stage as a launch pad, *Apollo 11* lifted off the Moon in a cloud of fine dust.

A short flight and careful maneuvering brought the lunar module level with the command module. Collins had been piloting this in orbit around the Moon all the time Armstrong and Aldrin had been on the surface. The two craft docked, allowing the lunar astronauts to be reunited with their colleague. After casting off from the unneeded lunar module, the crew fired their main engine to break out of orbit and begin the long journey home.

⊕ With the Earth in the background, the lunar module's ascent stage nears the orbiting command module.

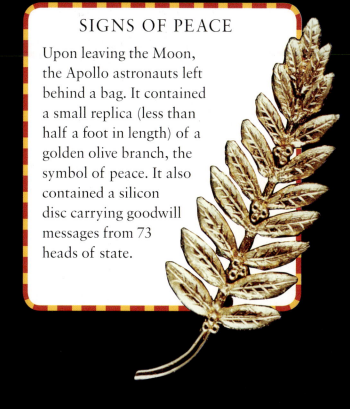

SIGNS OF PEACE

Upon leaving the Moon, the Apollo astronauts left behind a bag. It contained a small replica (less than half a foot in length) of a golden olive branch, the symbol of peace. It also contained a silicon disc carrying goodwill messages from 73 heads of state.

DID YOU KNOW . . . MOON FACTS . . .

Abandoned in lunar orbit, the ascent stage crashed into the Moon's surface years later.

THE DARK SIDE

Long before anyone made a horror film, folktales spoke of the terrible things that happened when the Moon was full. This was the evil time, when loathsome creatures appeared out of the shadows, when normally gentle human beings were transformed into uncontrollable beasts thirsting for the warm blood of the innocent.

WEREWOLVES

The most dangerous creature associated with the Moon is the werewolf. This is a man who, always at night and usually when the Moon is full, changes himself into a wolf. In countries where wolves are not common, the "shape-shifter" may become a tiger, bear, or other wild animal. Whatever form they take, "werecreatures" are normally vicious.

The happiest breeding ground for werewolves appears to have been sixteenth-century France, where dozens of people were accused. Two centuries later, the Beast of Gévaudan killed around 80 men, women, and children. Wolf, serial killer . . . or werewolf? All we know is that after several wolves in the Gévaudan area were hunted down and killed, the attacks stopped.

⬆ The film *Underworld* (2003) featured a moonlit fantasy war between werewolves and vampires.

⬆ The Beast of Gévaudan.

POSSESSED

Patients suffering from the mental illness lycanthropy believe they really are a wolf or other animal. In the past, those afflicted with this delusion were burned alive for being possessed by evil spirits.

SHAPE-SHIFTING

Some people became werewolves deliberately, by making a pact with the Devil. Others shape-shifted in error, perhaps by drinking from a magic spring or falling in love with another werewolf. Whatever the reason, when the Moon rose full and bright, their hair began to grow, their mouth stretched into a muzzle, and their voice distorted into a dreadful howl.

The link between vampires and the Moon is a modern invention. Traditionally, bloodsucking vampires came out at night, whether there was a Moon or not. The movie industry added a full Moon to the scene because of the Moon's association with werewolves and its cold, eerie light.

● New lunacy: The link between the Moon and bloodsucking vampires was created by the movie industry.

SPLASHDOWN!

The service module was discarded just before *Apollo 11* reentered the Earth's atmosphere. Now alone, the tiny manned command module plunged earthward, generating surface temperatures of 2,760°F (1,516°C). The astronauts were saved by its sturdy heat shield, which glowed white hot but did not transmit heat to the rest of the craft.

RECOVERY

As *Apollo 11* sped through the upper atmosphere, its 12 mini rockets kept it level and on course. Once down to 4,536 miles (7,300 km), a first set of small parachutes were let out. These slowed the module enough for three large parachutes to be opened at an altitude of 2,050 miles (3,300 km), braking the module to a leisurely 21.7 mph (35 km/h) by the time it splashed down into the Pacific Ocean. Here, three air balloons made sure the module was upright, and a buoyant orange collar around the edge helped keep it afloat. An hour later, the first helicopter arrived and lifted Armstrong, Aldrin, and Collins to safety. Their battered craft was rescued later.

❷ Safety first: The command module is disinfected as the three astronauts, now in biological suits, wait to be taken to a nearby rescue vessel.

⬆ You OK in there? US President Richard Nixon jokes with the astronauts, isolated in their mobile quarantine facility.

GLORY DAYS

Airlifted to the waiting USS *Hornet*, the three lunar astronauts were welcomed like heroes. Even President Nixon was on board to greet them. There was just one snag — in case they had brought back some unknown bug or virus, they were kept in sterile isolation for almost three weeks. After this, the red carpet was really rolled out. There were city parades, banquets, medal ceremonies, and endless handshakes, interviews, and speeches all over the United States. Then followed a 45-day world tour that took them to 25 countries and meetings with a glittering array of kings, queens, and presidents. The men from the Moon had become the most famous people on Earth.

DID YOU KNOW... MOON FACTS

Without a heat shield, on reentering Earth's atmosphere the command module would have burned up in seconds.

⬆ *Hola!* An enthusiastic Mexican crowd greets the *Apollo* astronauts during their world tour.

THE MOON AS A SYMBOL

The crescent Moon is one of the world's most easily recognized symbols. It can be found everywhere, from prehistoric cave carvings to modern national flags. An emblem of one of the world's great religions, it is also tattooed onto bodies and fashioned into elegant jewelry. In short, we love the Moon!

◈ Moon rock: a carving of the crescent Moon with a human face.

CRESCENT CITIES

The waxing crescent Moon (curving to the left; see pages 58–59) was a widely used symbol of ancient gods. Perhaps because it was associated with the goddess Diana, the crescent was adopted by the city of Constantinople (modern-day Istanbul). Alternatively, it may have been a thank-you to the Moon for coming out suddenly and saving the city from a surprise attack. The same shape — this time representing a loop in the Mississippi river — has also served as a symbol of New Orleans, Louisiana, USA.

MOON FLAGS

At least 14 countries have a crescent Moon somewhere on their national flag. A red crescent is also the emblem of the National Red Crescent Societies, partners of the Red Cross.

MUSLIM MOON

The crescent Moon became an Islamic symbol only quite recently. The idea came through the Ottoman Turks. These Muslim people were using the crescent motif by the mid-fourteenth century, although no one is quite sure what the sign meant to them. It may have represented a pair of claws or horns. Later, thanks to Turkish domination of the Muslim world, the lunar motif gradually became associated with Islam.

ARTY MOON

In popular Western culture — in body art, for example — the Moon has another set of meanings. It represents the female side of our nature, the intuitive and psychic. Other cultures claim it as a symbol of heaven and of the child that lurks within everyone, no matter what their age.

And all this from what is, in reality, no more than a distant lump of dead rock!

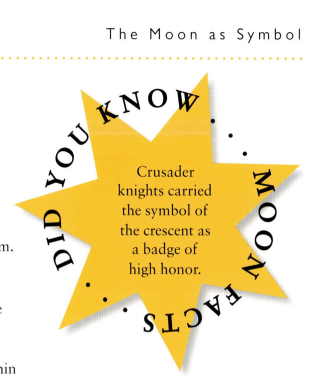

DID YOU KNOW . . . . MOON FACTS

Crusader knights carried the symbol of the crescent as a badge of high honor.

⊙ A wall painting at Luxor, Egypt, shows the crescent Moon hanging over Mecca, Islam's holiest city.

ART AND SCIENCE

Artists have always been fascinated by the Moon. Since civilization began, they have reproduced it in carvings, paintings, and drawings. For much of this time, art was closely linked to science: Before the invention of photography, sculpture, drawing, and painting were the only ways of recording how things looked.

PICTURING THE MOON

The Moon was first examined through a telescope around 1608. What a shock those early astronomers had! Instead of a nice shiny face, they saw a grim landscape of mountains and craters. Galileo (see page 35), who fortunately was a skilled artist, made his dramatic drawings of the lunar surface after examining it with a telescope that magnified 20 times.

Some 200 years later, John William Draper obtained the earliest photograph of the Moon using a telescope. Millions of photos followed, but their precision was limited by the distortion caused by the Earth's atmosphere. It was only when the Russians and Americans rose above the atmosphere that we were finally able to capture our mysterious neighbor close-up.

BEAUTIFUL BLEND

Five of Galileo's watercolor paintings of the Moon were rediscovered only recently. A beautiful blend of art and science, they show its bumpy surface and how sunlight normally illuminates just part of the lunar landscape.

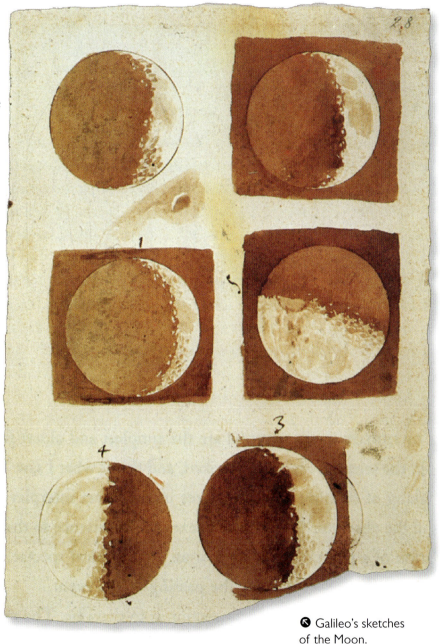

Galileo's sketches of the Moon.

⊘ The Moon as a symbol of purity in *The Immaculate Conception* by Bartolomé Murillo.

CHANGING VISIONS

In much early art the Moon was a symbol included in pictures to represent something else. In Christian paintings, for instance, it stood for purity, and many early pictures of the Virgin Mary, Jesus' mother, had a Moon in them. This was fine as long as the Moon looked pure — bright and shining and white.

Then, in the early seventeenth century, came Galileo and his telescope. . . . All of a sudden the Moon did not look quite so pure! In close-up, it was shown to be pockmarked and ugly — not really a suitable symbol for the Virgin Mother. Thanks to science, Christian artists had to look around for a more suitable symbol.

PAINTED MOON

In recent times, several painters have explored the differences between how the world appears in daylight and by moonlight. Van Gogh's painting *Evening Landscape with Rising Moon* is a fine example. More abstract but just as exciting is *Simultaneous Contrasts: Sun and Moon* by Robert Delaunay.

A BLACK-AND-WHITE WORLD

Just why does the world look different by moonlight? Part of the explanation is the construction of the human eye. At its back lies a sort of screen dotted with millions of receptors known as "rods" and "cones" that tell the brain when they are picking up light. The rods are extremely light-sensitive but do not register color. The cones, on the other hand, distinguish colors but are not very sensitive. In moonlight we rely heavily on the rods, which is why the nighttime world appears largely colorless.

⬅ *Moonlit Landscape* by Van Gogh (1889).

DID YOU KNOW . . . MOON FACTS

Unlike human beings and honeybees, moths can see in color by pale moonlight.

DARK LIGHT

As filmmakers know, moonlight gives a special atmosphere. The painter Henri Rousseau used it to subdue his colors and give his work a strange, sinister feel. In his younger days, the French artist Georges Seurat did something similar. Marc Chagall even gave the Moon a face in his disturbing picture *Russian Village Under the Moon*.

Today's artists use the Moon's shape and light just as their predecessors did. The Russian Igor Avramenko often has a Moon in his paintings, even if it is not always the right way up, and the American Lise Carlson has painted the Moon as seen by a turtle looking up from beneath the water.

Whether as symbol, source of special light, or as part of the natural world, clearly the Moon's power to fire our imagination is as strong as ever.

NOSTALGIC MOON

The last work of the famous Japanese artist Tsukioka Yoshitoshi was *One Hundred Aspects of the Moon*. These late-nineteenth-century prints reflect traditional Japanese culture, before it came under Western influence.

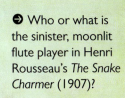

➲ Who or what is the sinister, moonlit flute player in Henri Rousseau's *The Snake Charmer* (1907)?

RETURN TO THE MOON

The *Apollo* program saw six further Moon shots and five landings. The activities became increasingly ambitious. More and heavier samples of rock and surface material were brought back, and astronauts explored widely in Lunar Roving Vehicles. It was all hugely expensive, however, and by 1975 the program was over.

LIGHTNING AND EXPLOSION

After taking off in a thunderstorm, *Apollo 12* was struck by lightning and for a moment it looked as if the mission might have to be aborted. It was saved by the crew's quick thinking. Astronaut Alan L. Bean was thinking less carefully when he pointed the mission's color TV camera directly at the Sun, causing it to burn out.

Apollo 13, the subject of a popular movie, never made a Moon landing because of an explosion in one of the service module's oxygen tanks on the way out. Despite early docking difficulties and computer problems, *Apollo 14* went well. So large were the samples collected that the crew needed a "lunar rickshaw" to carry them around.

↑ Lightning strikes during the launch of *Apollo 12*.

"SUCCESSFUL FAILURE"

The three *Apollo 13* astronauts lived for four days in a lunar module designed to sustain two people for two days. When they returned to Earth alive, Mission Control labeled the venture a "successful failure."

◑ Handyman: astronaut John Swigert with the home-made device he and other members of the *Apollo 13* crew constructed to save their lives.

BUGGY BOYS

After the pioneering work of the early lunar landings, the ninth manned mission (*Apollo 15*) placed much greater emphasis on science. It carried a range of new equipment, including highly sophisticated cameras. More exciting was the Lunar Roving Vehicle or "Moon Buggy," a battery-powered jeep capable of traveling 11 mph (18 km/h). Bouncing along in it, David Scott and James Irwin traveled several miles from the landing site during their three days on the Moon.

The last two missions took the scientific work even further. *Apollo 16* was the first to land in a highland area, while *Apollo 17* included geologist Harrison Schmitt, the first trained scientist to serve as an astronaut.

⬎ Let's go! David R. Scott driving off in *Apollo 15*'s "Moon Buggy."

ALAN L. BEAN

Astronaut and *Apollo 12* pilot Alan L. Bean (b. 1932) spent 1,671 hours in space. Filled with wonder for the Universe, he felt words and photos did not do it justice. So, after retiring in 1981, he devoted his time to painting.

"Whoopee! Man, that may have been a small one for Neil, but that's a long one for me."

APOLLO 12 ASTRONAUT PETE CONRAD AS HE STEPPED ONTO THE MOON

LIVING ON THE MOON

We're going back! In 2006 NASA announced that it hoped to return human beings to the Moon by 2020 and enable them to live there for months at a time by 2024. And after that? Scientists and engineers are already producing plans for lunar cities under gigantic glass domes. . . .

PAVING THE WAY

Before the proposed 2020 landing, there will be dozens of unmanned missions to increase our knowledge of the Moon and how we might live there. Some of these projects will use conventional rockets, others will try out different power sources.

The European Space Agency plans an ion-engined craft driven by solar power. Another idea is to fire special shells. These would plunge deep into the lunar surface then send back information on the surrounding environment.

⊕ Fantasy into reality: an artist's impression of life in a lunar city.

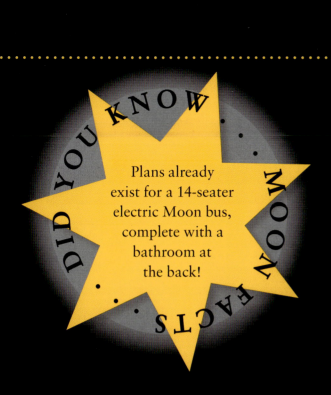

Plans already exist for a 14-seater electric Moon bus, complete with a bathroom at the back!

MOON BASE

The next Moon landing craft will probably be a sort of lunar caravan in which astronauts will live and work for several weeks. Some kind of semipermanent base will come next, built by a multinational team. At the moment, scientists suggest the lunar South Pole as the best site. It has sunlight nearly all the time, and deep under the surface there may even be frozen water.

MOON FARM

To solve the problem of 655 hours of uninterrupted sunlight, a floating Moon farm under a half-transparent and half-blacked-out dome has been suggested. By revolving 360 degrees every 24 hours, it would re-create Earth-style days and nights.

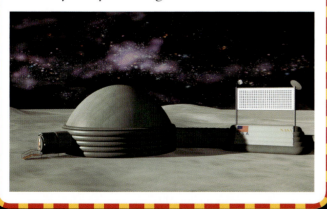

LUNAR MANUFACTURE

Ferrying up from Earth everything needed for a Moon settlement would be impossibly costly and wasteful. The answer is to make the Moon base as self-sufficient as possible. Essentially, this means harnessing solar energy to produce oxygen, food, and materials.

The Moon's plentiful silica may be used to construct a vast, airtight double-glazed greenhouse. Next, specially bred microbes are introduced, then plants. Between them they create an atmosphere capable of sustaining earthly life.

Anyone for a Moon vacation?

⬆ Jetting to the Moon: Films and TV shows like *The Jetsons* have been anticipating lunar lifestyles for decades.

UNSEEN INFLUENCE

Astrologers believe that the position of the Moon, together with that of the Sun, planets, and stars, influences what happens to human beings. In particular, they claim that celestial bodies determine what sort of person we are — and our luck. These are worked out from a chart known as a "horoscope."

MOON SIGN

A typical horoscope appearing every day in newspapers and magazines and on Web sites is based on the Sun. Where the Sun was at the time of our birth gives us our Sun sign, often called "star sign." There are 12 of these, such as Gemini, Capricorn, Aries, and so forth. However, according to astrologers, we also have a Moon sign.

The Moon sign is more difficult to figure out because it involves knowing where the fast-moving Moon was in relation to all other major celestial bodies at the time we were born. With this information, astrologers produce a "birth chart" that sets out a person's character and how they should live.

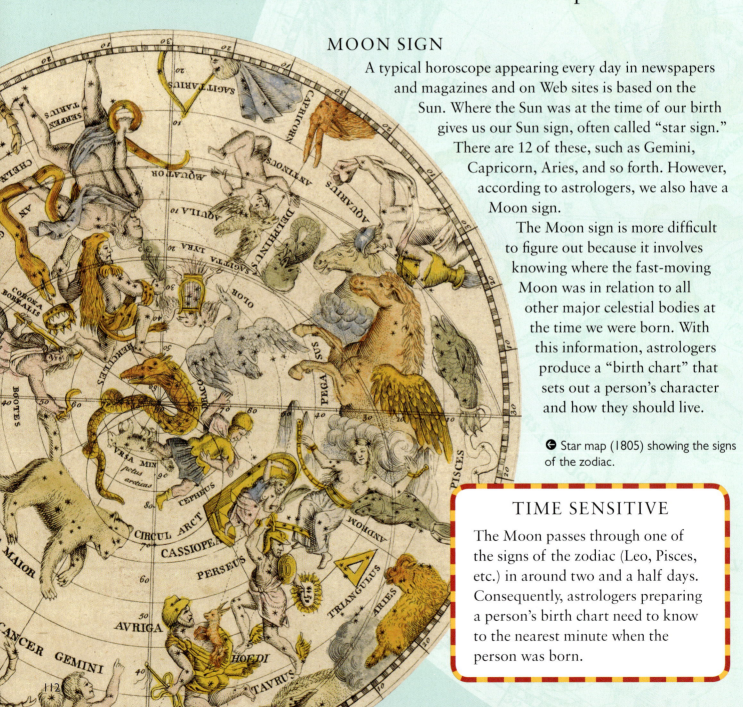

◑ Star map (1805) showing the signs of the zodiac.

TIME SENSITIVE

The Moon passes through one of the signs of the zodiac (Leo, Pisces, etc.) in around two and a half days. Consequently, astrologers preparing a person's birth chart need to know to the nearest minute when the person was born.

❼ Pisces the fish, a "water" sign hand-painted on an early modern tile.

TWO PERSONALITIES

Our Sun sign is said to be our "outer" personality — the side of us that we show to others. Thus, people born under the sign of Aries are supposed to be energetic and outgoing but rather impulsive.

Our Moon sign represents our "inner" personality — the side we keep hidden. This is the field of emotion, feelings, and heartfelt secrets. It may contrast strongly with the outer personality. For example, someone with an Aries Sun sign may have a Virgo Moon sign, making the inner personality logical, clear-headed, and well-organized. This, say astrologers, explains why human beings are so complicated.

"Those born with the Moon in a Water sign need to establish solid emotional commitments."

MOON IN PISCES
HOROSCOPE,
JUNE 9, 2008

LUNAR DATING

> The full Moon illuminates a minaret on a mosque.

The Moon's glorious mystery has inspired wonder and worship, paintings and drawings, songs and symphonies, love and loss, fairy tales and horror movies, calendars, horoscopes, rituals, and festivals. Apart from the great Sun itself, no other single object has had an impact on the human imagination as powerfully as the Moon.

LIGHT IN THE DARKNESS

Once humans had settled in communities, they needed to organize their lives. To provide the necessary framework, they devised calendars based around the single day. The next step was to gather groups of days into weeks and months. This involved the Moon.

> Date data: a calendar from ancient Rome.

THE GREAT PROBLEM

All early calendar makers faced the same problem:
• A year is the time the Earth takes to orbit the Sun: 365 days (actually 365.242199 days).
• A traditional month is the time it takes the Moon to go through all its phases: 29.5 days (actually 29.53059 days).

But a lunar year of 354 (12 x 29.5) days does not fit with the solar year! What to do?

The obvious answer was to pad out the calendar with extra days. At first this meant adopting a system of months of 29 and 30 days alternately. The system of one month (February) of 28 or 29 days and others of 30 or 31 days was introduced by

"[He] . . . in the course of one revolving Moon, Was chemist, fiddler, statesman, and buffoon."

JOHN DRYDEN
DESCRIBING GEORGE
VILLIERS, 2ND DUKE OF
BUCKINGHAM, 1681

HIPPARCHUS

The ancient Greek astronomer Hipparchus (c. 150 BCE) listed 1,080 stars, invented trigonometry, and calculated the lunar month at 29.53058 days — off by just 0.00001.

RELIGIOUS CALENDARS

Islam, Christianity, Hinduism, Buddhism, and many other religions use a lunar-based calendar. That is why, for instance, the date of the Christian Easter changes from year to year. The Muslim calendar is entirely Moon-based. Its months alternate between 29 and 30 days, and a year is 354 or 355 days. Each month starts with the sighting of the new Moon. As a consequence, in 2008 the fasting month of Ramadan began on September 1 in the Middle East (September 2 in North America), while in 2010 it will begin on August 11.

MOONBEAMS

The *Apollo* program was but one step on a never-ending journey. One day we will know the Moon as well as we know Earth. We will understand its composition and how it was created. We will live there, exploit its resources, and make it a base for further exploration. Yet still the magic will remain.

THE GREAT EXPEDITION

What an expedition we have been on! It began all those millennia ago with our distant ancestors gazing up at the Moon in awe and wonder, and worshipping its glory.

Then came the thinkers — those who devoted their lives to figuring out exactly what the heavens were and how they operated. They were followed by the explorers: the rocket makers, astrophysicists, astronauts, and cosmonauts.

In 1969, the wheel turned full circle. The story that had started with celestial gods returned to them: Apollo, the Sun god, roared from the Earth to greet his twin sister, Artemis, the Moon goddess.

◈ This famous view of Elliott with E.T. in his bicycle basket silhouetted against the Moon is recognized by children all over the world.

EVERLASTING INSPIRATION

All this time, to artists, astrologers, poets, playwrights, and composers, the Moon was a source of endless inspiration. Perhaps surprisingly, our growing scientific knowledge did not reduce the Moon's power to fire the passions of both good and evil. In fact, through cinema, popular song, and science fiction, the Moon is possibly a more powerful image today than it has ever been. Just as the real, physical Moon is always there, so is its twin in the human imagination.

The Stars and Stripes wave good luck as *Apollo 11* roars by on course for the Moon and its place in history.

"We'll go no more a-roving
So late into the night,
Though the heart be still as loving,
And the moon be still as bright."

LORD BYRON, 1817

OUR MOON

So there we have it — our Moon, with its dark side as well as its light; reliable yet unreliable; often glorious yet sometimes terrifying; understood, misunderstood, and eternally mysterious. . . .

And the key to this enduring fascination? Why, the Moon is just like us!

MOON INFO

GENERAL

The brightest object in our sky after the Sun.

Has no proper name, just "the Moon" (there are many other moons in space).

Owned by no one.

A lifeless, rocky sphere.

NUMBERS

Mean distance from Earth: 238,855 miles (384,400 km)

Orbits Earth: every 27.3 days.

Time between full Moons: 29.5 days.

Orbits the Sun: in one year (as does Earth).

Size in relation to Earth: approx. one-quarter.

Radius at Equator: 1,080 miles (1,738 km).

Center of mass: 1.2 miles (2 km) from geometric center.

Density: 0.007 pounds per cubic inch (3.34 g per cubic cm).

Volume: 2% of Earth's.

Mass: 0.0123 of Earth's.

Gravity: one-sixth Earth's.

Surface area: 0.074 Earth's.

Surface visible from Earth: 59%.

Surface temperature: between 253°F (123°C) and -387°F (-233°C).

Moving away from Earth: at 1.5 inches (3.8 cm) per year.

Time between eclipses: approx. 18 years and 11 months.

MOON MISCELLANY

Made up of an outer crust, mantle, and core.

No magnetic field, no seasons, and negligible atmosphere.

Revolves at the same rate as it circles the Earth, so we see only one side.

Orbit around Earth is slightly eccentric.

Once volcanic, so most rocks are igneous (formed by cooling lava).

Surface made of rocks and dust.

Main features are *maria* ("seas" of cooled lava), highlands, and valleys.

Pockmarked appearance is a result of continual bombardment by large and small particles from space.

Contains tiny amounts of water.

Eclipses when Earth, Moon, and Sun are aligned: (a) lunar eclipse, when Earth blots out the Sun's light on the Moon; (b) solar eclipse, when the Moon comes between Earth and the Sun.

LUNAR EXPLORATION

Soviet *Luna 2* first craft to reach Moon (1959).

Soviet *Luna 3* first craft to photograph dark side of Moon (1959).

Soviet *Luna 9* first craft to soft land on Moon (1966).

Soviet *Luna 10* first craft to orbit Moon (1966).

US *Apollo 8* first manned craft to circle Moon (1969).

US *Apollo 11* lands first humans on Moon (1969).

US *Apollo 17* carries last humans to visit Moon (1972).

APOLLO PROGRAM

Launched May 1961

1961, Oct	SA-1 [*Apollo 1*]: first test flight of *Saturn* rocket.*
1962, Apr	*Apollo 2*: test flight of *Saturn* rocket.
1962, Nov	*Apollo 3*: another *Saturn* test launch.
*1967, Jan	*Apollo 1*: spacecraft caught fire on ground; three astronauts killed. Mission named *Apollo 1* in honor of those who died.
1967, Nov	*Apollo 4*: first launch of *Saturn V* rocket.
1968, Jan	*Apollo 5*: unmanned flight to test lunar module in space.
1968, Apr	*Apollo 6*: last unmanned test launch of *Saturn V*.
1968, Oct	*Apollo 7*: three-man crew into orbit.
1968, Dec	*Apollo 8*: three-man crew orbit Moon.
1969, Mar	*Apollo 9*: three-man crew in 10-day orbit testing all modules to be used for Moon landing.
1969, May	*Apollo 10*: dummy run for Moon landing.
1969, Jul	*Apollo 11*: first Moon landing.
1969, Nov	*Apollo 12*: return to Moon.
1970, Apr	*Apollo 13*: "successful failure" after explosion on board.
1971, Jan–Feb	*Apollo 14*: uses "lunar rickshaw."
1971, Jul–Aug	*Apollo 15*: three days on Moon.
1972, Apr	*Apollo 16*: lands in highlands area.
1972, Dec	*Apollo 17*: last manned visit to Moon.

➲ Historic walk: The three *Apollo 11* astronauts make their way to the launchpad.

APOLLO 11

Mission Control: Houston, Texas, USA.

Launch: Kennedy Space Center, Florida, USA, July 16, 1969.

Lunar landing: Sea of Tranquility, July 20.

Splashdown: Pacific Ocean, July 24.

Crew: Neil Armstrong (commander); Edwin "Buzz" Aldrin (LM pilot); Michael Collins (CM).

Rocket: three-stage *Saturn V* with fully laden explosive power of atomic bomb.

Modules: unmanned service module, command module *Columbia* (CSM 66,844 pounds [30,320 kg]), two-part lunar module *Eagle* (36,262 pounds [16,448 kg]).

Time on lunar surface: 21 hrs 36 mins.

MOON DATES

c. 4.5 billion BCE	The Moon is formed.

3500 BCE	Several ancient civilizations worship Moon deities.
c. 3200 BCE	Rock carving made at Knowth, Ireland, may be the earliest picture of the Moon.
c. 464 BCE	Greek philosopher Anaxagoras teaches that the Moon receives its light from the Sun.
46 BCE	Julius Caesar introduces the Julian calendar, with 12 months and a leap day every fourth February.
c. 150 CE	Greek philosopher Ptolemy sets out his theory of an Earth-centered universe. This is accepted in the Christian and Muslim worlds for many centuries.
c. 165 CE	Lucian writes the first sci-fi book, *True Story*, about a trip to the Moon.
622 CE	Beginning of the Islamic lunar calendar.
c. 1010	Muslim scholar al-Biruni suggests the idea of gravity and offers a scientific explanation for the phases of the Moon.
c. 1180	Muslim scholar ibn-Rushd (Averroës) rejects Ptolemy's theory of the Universe.
c. 1250	The Chinese make the first rockets.
15th century	Muslim Ottoman Turks adopt the crescent Moon and star as their flag.
1543	Polish astronomer Nicolaus Copernicus publishes his scientific theory of a Sun-centered universe.
1595	John Lyly's play *Woman in the Moon*.
1596–1619	German astronomer Johannes Kepler offers a scientific explanation of the movement of celestial bodies.

1609	Galileo Galilei begins his observation of the Moon through a telescope.
1687	Newton's principles of motion and theory of gravity explain the Moon's behavior scientifically.
1764–67	A werewolflike beast terrorizes Gévaudan, France.
1801	Ludwig van Beethoven writes the piano sonata that will be renamed *Moonlight*.
1804	William Congreve designs a rocket capable of being aimed accurately.
c. 1840	The Moon is first photographed through a telescope.
1865	Jules Verne writes his novel *From the Earth to the Moon*.
1889	Vincent Van Gogh paints *Evening Landscape with Rising Moon*.
1901	H. G. Wells writes his novel *The First Men in the Moon*.
1902	French film *A Trip to the Moon* released.
1903	Claude Debussy composes *Clair de Lune*.
1919	American scientist Robert H. Goddard publishes his rocket treatise *A Method of Reaching Extreme Altitudes*.
1934	Richard Rodgers and Lorenz Hart write the famous song "Blue Moon."
1944	The first V2 rockets hit London.
1950	Sci-fi movies *Rocketship X-M* and *Destination Moon* are released.
1954	Comic-book hero Tintin goes to the Moon.
1957	The Soviets launch the first man-made satellite, *Sputnik I*.
1958	NASA is formed.

1959, Jan	Soviet *Luna 1* gets within about 3,728 miles (6,000 km) of the Moon.
1959, May	The US sends two monkeys into orbit.
1959, Oct	Soviet *Luna 3* sends back the first pictures of the far side of the Moon.
1961, Apr	Yuri Gagarin of the USSR becomes the world's first spaceman.
1961, May	Alan Shepard becomes the first American astronaut.
1961, May	US President John F. Kennedy announces that the US will put a man on the Moon by the end of the decade.
1961, Oct	The *Saturn I* rocket is first launched.
1962	John Glenn becomes the first American to orbit Earth.
1963	Russian Valentina Tereshkova becomes the first spacewoman.
1964, Jan	US *Ranger 6* reaches the Moon.
1965, Mar	Soviet cosmonaut Alexei Leonov becomes the first man to walk in space.
1966, Jan	Soviet *Luna 9* makes the first soft landing on the Moon.
1966, May	US *Surveyor 1* makes a soft landing on the Moon.

1967, Jan	The crew of *Apollo 1* dies in a fire during training.
1967, Nov	The *Saturn V* rocket makes its first flight (*Apollo 4*).
1968, Oct	First manned *Apollo* mission (no. 7).
1968, Dec	*Apollo 8* orbits the Moon.
1969, Mar	*Apollo 9* tests the lunar module in space.
1969, May	*Apollo 10* comes close to the lunar surface before returning to Earth.
1969, Jul	*Apollo 11* lands men on the Moon for the first time and returns successfully.
1969, Nov	*Apollo 12*: the second US visit to the Moon.

1970, Apr	The *Apollo 13* mission returns to Earth early after an explosion on board.
1970, Sep	The unmanned Soviet *Luna 16* returns to Earth with samples from the Moon.
1970, Nov	The unmanned Soviet *Luna 17* lands a rover on the Moon.
1971, Jan–Feb	*Apollo 14*: the third successful Moon landing and return.
1971, Jul–Aug	*Apollo 15* uses a rover to explore the Moon.
1972, Apr	*Apollo 16*: the penultimate manned Moon landing.

1972, Dec	*Apollo 17*: the last manned lunar mission.
1975	The *Apollo* program ends.
1979	Ian Fleming publishes his James Bond novel *Moonraker*.
1990	The Japanese launch a rocket into lunar orbit.
1993	Harold Pinter's play *Moonlight* is written.
1994	The US *Clementine* maps the lunar surface.
1998	The US *Lunar Prospector* begins a survey of the Moon's surface for a possible site for a base.
2003	The European Space Agency sends *Smart 1* into lunar orbit.
2006	The US proposes to return to the Moon by 2020, with a colony set up there by 2024.
2007	China launches a lunar orbiter.

GLOSSARY

abstract art art concerned with shapes, colors, and patterns rather than lifelike images

annular ring-shaped

astrology fortune-telling by observation of celestial bodies

astronaut human space traveler

astronomer one who studies celestial bodies from Earth

astrophysicist scientist who specializes in the physics of the Universe

atmosphere gas and other particles surrounding a celestial body such as the Moon

barycenter center of gravity

celestial body any large object found in space

Celts peoples who spread across Western Europe in late prehistoric times

centrifugal force force that drives objects away from the point they are circling

Columbia name given to the *Apollo 11* command module

colony settlement away from the motherland

command module main section of *Apollo 11* in which astronauts traveled to and from the Moon

Communism system of government in which individual ambitions are less important than the community (normally the state)

constellation group of stars

core central part of a celestial body

Corporal small US rocket used in the 1950s and 1960s

cosmonaut Russian word for an astronaut

crescent sickle-shaped

crusader medieval Christian warrior who attempted to recapture the Holy Places in the Middle East from Muslims

crust solid outer layer of a celestial body

data information, usually in the form of facts and figures

dehydrated without the usual amount of water

dock joining together in space of two or more units of equipment

Eagle name given to *Apollo 11's* lunar module

eclipse when one celestial body regularly comes between another two, obscuring their view of each other

element one of the basic atoms from which all known substances are made

ellipse path in the form of a distorted circle

equinox biannual time when day and night are of equal length

ethanol ethyl alcohol, the form of alcohol found in alcoholic drinks, also used as a fuel

gantry supporting framework of metal girders

Gemini US 12-flight program of two-man spaceflights in the 1960s

ghoul demon that preys on the dead

gibbous fat or swollen, used to describe the Moon between its half and full stages

gravity force of attraction between two particles, one of which is usually a celestial body such as Earth

hatch small door that can be sealed

heat shield ultra-tough dish protecting a space vehicle as it reenters Earth's atmosphere

hemisphere half a sphere

horoscope set of astrological predictions

hypothesis unconfirmed theory

ibis deerlike creature with large horns

impact collision

inert nonreactive

intuitive inspired by guesswork

Inuit peoples inhabiting the Arctic regions

ion electronically charged atom or charged free subatomic particle

kerosene type of fuel, also known as paraffin

Korean War war between North and South Korea (1950–53) in which other nations joined

Latin language of the ancient Roman civilization

lava liquid rock released by volcanoes

lunar of the Moon

lunar module two-part section of *Apollo 11* that landed on and took off from the Moon

maelstrom mighty whirlpool or any state of extreme confusion and chaos

malevolence evil

mantle layer of a celestial body beneath the outer crust

mare sealike feature on the Moon's surface

mass the amount of matter in an object

Mesopotamia modern-day Iraq

meteor small piece of debris flying through space and burning brightly in Earth's atmosphere

mission targeted task

molten normally solid substance in liquid form

moonstone pearly gemstone

myth story with no foundation in truth

NASA US National Aeronautics and Space Administration, founded 1958

neap tide tide with smallest difference between high and low water

orbit path of an object around a celestial body

penumbra lighter shadow around the central dark shadow of an eclipse

phase of the Moon one of the shapes through which the Moon regularly passes

PhD doctor of philosophy

phenomenon unusual occurrence

philosopher someone who seeks the truths behind all things

planet celestial body that orbits a star

polka type of dance

primeval at the beginning of time

propaganda inaccurate or slanted information intended to put over a particular point of view

psychic belonging to the realm of the mind or soul, beyond the physical

Ranger unmanned US lunar program of the 1960s

rational according to reason

Redstone early US rocket developed from German V2 used in the Second World War

rille dry furrow or riverlike feature on the Moon's surface

satellite object, often man-made, that orbits a celestial body

Saturn huge rocket that lifted the *Apollo* missions beyond Earth's gravitational field

sci-fi science fiction

service module rocket-powered section of *Apollo 11* that housed its supplies

sign of the zodiac constellation with a shape that, fancifully, represents an earthly object, such as Leo (Lion) and Gemini (twins)

Solar System Sun and its planets

sonata piece of music with a distinct form or pattern

Soviet relating to the USSR

spring tide tide with the largest difference between high and low water

Sputnik first man-made satellite, launched by the USSR in 1957

static electricity electric charge not in the form of a current

Sumer earliest Mesopotamian civilization

Surveyor unmanned NASA program of the 1960s that surveyed the lunar surface

umbra shade

USSR Union of Soviet Socialist Republics, the Russian-based Communist empire, 1924–91

vampire mythical bloodsucking creature

velocity rate of motion in a specific direction

Vostok Soviet rocket and space program of the 1960s

wane get smaller

wax get larger

werewolf human that turns into a wolf when the Moon is full

zombie corpse brought back to life (myth)

INDEX

Page numbers in **bold** indicate pictures.

MOON SITES

GENERAL

Those undertaking Internet moonsearch of their own are strongly advised to start with one of the impartial, objective, online encyclopedias such as:

www.britannica.com

www.worldbookonline.com

www.infoplease.com/encyclopedia

Beware free information sources! You are not guaranteed objectivity, reliability, or an appropriate academic level.

More specifically for science, try:

www.oup.co.uk/oxed/children/oise

www.accessscience.com

SPACE

The place to start is the amazingly comprehensive NASA site:
www.nasa.gov/home
NASA is funded by the US government.

The European Space Agency site offers a slightly different perspective:
www.esa.int/esaCP/index.html

This site is full of up-to-date information:
www.spacedaily.com

See also:

www.solarviews.com

www.russianspaceweb.com

www.space.com

http://history.nasa.gov

http://news.bbc.co.uk/onthisday/hi/themes/
science_and_technology/space

SCIENCE

The BBC:

www.bbc.co.uk/science/space/solarsystem/earth/
moon.shtml

The Science Museum, London
www.sciencemuseum.org.uk

The Smithsonian, Washington, DC
http://www.si.edu/

CULTURE

Some other interesting sites:

http://home.hiwaay.net/~krcool/Astro/moon

www.skyscript.co.uk/moon.html

www.inconstantmoon.com/not_mus.htm

www.windows.ucar.edu/tour/link=/mythology/
planets/Earth/moon.html

www.moonlightsys.com/themoon/tunes.html

Ask an adult to help you find additional Web sites and check them out before you use them.

PLACES TO VISIT

Europe
National Space Centre, Leicester, UK (www.spacecentre.co.uk)
Toulouse Space Museum, Toulouse, France
 (www.cite-espace.com)
Euro Space Center, Belgium (www.eurospacecenter.be)

Americas
Johnson Space Center, Houston, Texas (www.spacecenter.org)
National Air and Space Museum, Smithsonian, Washington,
 DC (www.nasm.si.edu)
H. R. MacMillan Space Centre, Vancouver, Canada
 (www.hrmacmillanspacecentre.com)

Kennedy Space Center, Florida, US (http://www.
 kennedyspacecenter.com)
US Space & Rocket Center, Huntsville, Alabama, US
 (www. spacecamp.com)

Asia
Hong Kong Space Museum (www.lcsd.gov.hk/CE/Museum/
 Space)
Tanegashima Space Center (TNSC), Japan (www.jaxa.jp)

Acknowledgments

ACKNOWLEDGMENTS

The publishers would like to thank the following for permission to use their material. Every care has been taken to trace copyright holders. However, if there have been unintentional omissions or failure to trace copyright holders, we apologize and will, if informed, endeavor to make corrections in any future edition.

KEY
t = top; m = middle; b = bottom; l = left; r = right

akg-images: 17 (James Morris), 18, 22 (Jean-Louis Nou), 30, 98l, 103 (Gérard Degeorge).

Bridgeman Art Library: 13 (Fairy Art Museum, Tokyo, Japan), 16 (Private Collection), 26 (Private Collection, Christie's Images), 40l (Private Collection, Archives Charmet), 68b (Beethoven Haus, Bonn, Germany, Giraudon), 68t (Private Collection, Archives Charmet), 105 (Museo de Bellas Artes, Seville, Spain), 106 (Museu de Arte, São Paulo, Brazil), 107b (Musée d'Orsay, Paris, France, Lauros/Giraudon).

Corbis: 12 (Philadelphia Museum of Art), 12–13 (Sanford/Agliolo), 19 (Michael Nicholson), 20 (Bettmann), 25t (Rykoff Collection), 27l (The Gallery Collection), 27r (Roger Antrobus), 29 (Roger Wood), 33 (Cynthia Hart), 34 (Paul Alamasy), 47 (Art Archive), 60l (Ajay Verma/Reuters), 62 (Tom Fox/*Dallas Morning News*), 64b (Bettmann), 73 (Marc Mueller/dpa), 86 (Swim Ink 2, LLC), 114 (Araldo de Luca), 115 (Bettmann).

Dreamstime: 67t (Redeyed), 67b (Gail Johnson), 102b (Cihan Demirok).

Getty: 24r (AFP), 92 (Time & Life Pictures), 102t (Chip Simons).

iStock: 32 (Chris Ronneseth), 32–33 (Stephen Inglis), 42–43, 48–49, 60r (Edward Karaa), 63b (Jan Rysavy), 66 (Jan Rysavy), 82–83, 82bl (Christine Balderas), 82br (Duncan Walker), 82tl, 82tr (Nic Taylor), 83l, 83r (Christine Balderas), 114–115 (Damir Cudic).

Kobal Collection: 52 (George Pal Prods), 53 (Lippert), 54 (Columbia), 55 (Melies), 69 (Focus Features), 72l (Polygram/Universal), 72r (Danjaq/Eon/UA), 87 (20th Century Fox), 98r (Subterranean/Screen Gems), 99 (Zoetrope/Columbia Tristar), 111r (Cuckoo's Nest/Hanna-Barbera/Wang Films), 116l (Universal/Kobal Collection).

Mary Evans Picture Library: 14, 14–15, 15, 23, 42 (Arthur Rackham), 43, 44, 44–45, 48l, 48r, 49, 61, 94, 95, 112, 113.

NASA: 63t; Great Images in NASA: 7, 9l, 9r, 21t, 21b, 24l, 36l, 36r, 37, 39t, 39b, 50l, 51, 56–57, 57, 64t, 65, 70, 71l, 77t, 78, 88l, 93, 97t, 101b, 101t, 108b, 109b, 117, 121l; Jet Propulsion Laboratory: 10–11, 46, 80t, 118–119; Johnson Space Center: 4–5, 58–59, 74b, 76mt, 76mb, 76bl, 76br, 76t, 77b, 79l, 79r, 81, 84, 85l, 85r, 89m, 89t, 90–91, 91t, 97b, 108m, 108t, 118, 121r; Kennedy Space Center: 2–3, 8t, 8bl, 8br, 91b, 96, 100, 109t, 119, 120b; Langley Research Center: 25b; Marshall Space Flight Center: 38.

Science Photo Library: 41 (Gary Hincks), 58–59 (David A. Hardy), 74 (Christian Darkin), 75 (Victor Habbick Visions), 80b (Chris Butler), 89b, 110 (Victor Habbick Visions), 111l (Friedrich Saurer), 120t (Detlev Van Ravenswaay).

Topfoto: 31 (Charles Walker), 40r.

Cover images: All images NASA. Front cover: Charles O'Rear/CORBIS, *A Carnival Evening* by Henri Rousseau (Philadelphia Museum of Art/CORBIS).

The author would like to thank the following for their kindness, patience, and assistance in the preparation of this book: Akum Gupta of the Mall School, Gill Denton of OUP, Steve White-Thomson of White-Thomson Publishing, and, especially, Sonya Newland of Big Blu Ltd. and indefatigable proofreader Lucy Ross.